Battleground

GAVRELLE

With the continued expansion of the Battleground series a **Battleground Europe Club** has been formed to benefit the reader. The purpose of the Club is to keep members informed of new titles and key developments by way of a quarterly newsletter, and to offer many other reader-benefits. Membership is free and by registering an interest you can help us predict print runs and thus maintain prices at their present levels. Please call the office 01226 734555, or send your name and address along with a request for more information to:

Battleground Europe Club Pen & Sword Books Ltd, 47 Church Street, Barnsley, South Yorkshire S70 2AS

Battleground Europe

GAVRELLE

TREVOR TASKER & KYLE TALLETT

Series editor
Nigel Cave

LEO COOPER

First published in 2000 by
LEO COOPER
an imprint of
Pen & Sword Books Limited
47 Church Street, Barnsley, South Yorkshire S70 2AS

ISBN 0 85052 688 4

A CIP catalogue of this book is available
from the British Library

Printed by Redwood Books Limited
Trowbridge, Wiltshire

*For up-to-date information on other titles produced under the Leo Cooper imprint,
please telephone or write to:*
Pen & Sword Books Ltd, FREEPOST, 47 Church Street
Barnsley, South Yorkshire S70 2AS
Telephone 01226 734222

ISRN

0850525209

BATTLE OF ARRAS

£19.95

JONATHAN NICHOLLS

PEN + SWORD BOOKS

BOOKSTACK   430554.

CONTENTS

The Windmill at Gavrelle. More Royal Marines fell around this mill than any other battlefield in the Corps' history. The mill was destroyed in 1917 and never rebuilt. Capron Family, Gavrelle

INTRODUCTION BY SERIES EDITOR

To be frank, the battlefield around Gavrelle is not situated in the most beautiful countryside on the Western Front - it is dominated by large, rather characterless fields and by a surfeit of high-speed roads and railway lines. Yet first impressions, in this case, are most certainly misleading. Kyle Tallett and Trevor Tasker have combined to make this neglected part of the Arras battlefield accessible to all those with an interest in the events of spring 1917 and of 1918.

Gavrelle is an important place in the history of that strangely British formation, the 63rd (Royal Naval) Division - in part because of the heavy fighting and casualties that they endured, in part because of the two Victoria Crosses that were won by the Division here. It is only fitting that such a fine memorial to these sailors-turned-soldiers should be positioned on the western edge of Gavrelle. Even at home interest in the RND has been such that soon it is hoped that the Divisional memorial will be restored to its original site on Horse Guards Parade.

A detailed study of Gavrelle should also illustrate to students of the Great War how much fighting methods on both sides, German and British, had evolved - even since the fighting on the Somme the previous year. Yet the stories of the small unit action and of the individual have not been lost, illustrated as they are by frequent use of personal reminiscences. Trevor Tasker has also been able to illustrate the complex story of the cemeteries that relate to the campaign and traced how particular people have found their final resting place in particular cemeteries.

The result of tremendous hard work, of relating trench maps to the ground today and of ferreting out information from a wide variety of British and French sources is a fascinating read. In addition, short chapters on the Second World War fighting and of individuals from that later fighting add a further dimension to the work.

No longer need the traveller on the N50 hurtle past a rather undistinguished village and a couple of wayside cemeteries and memorials, wondering how it figured in the conflicts of the twentieth century. This book is a great tribute to the combatants who fought and died for their countries in and around Gavrelle; and it enables us who come after them to keep their memory alive.

Nigel Cave
Derryswood July 2000

ACKNOWLEDGEMENTS

Many organisations and individuals have helped the authors in the production of this guide.

We would like to thank the Imperial War Museum (Photographic and Documents Departments), the Public Records Office at Kew, the Commonwealth War Graves Commission (CWGC) in Maidenhead and France, the Lancashire Fusiliers Museum (Bury), the Royal Marine Museum (Eastney), the Royal Air Force Museum (Hendon), Fleet Air Arm Museum (Yeovilton) and the National Archives of Canada (NAC) in Ottawa.

We would also like to thank Max Arthur; Steve Burgess; the Capron Family, (Gavrelle); Nigel Cave; Francis Dupayage, (Gavrelle); Tony Froom; Joseph Fouache, (Gavrelle); David Gruber; Roland Hernard, (Feuchy); Charles Hewitt; Shirley Hitchcock, (CWGC); Godfrey Owen James; Véronique Legrand, (pilote); Lequette Family, (Gavrelle); Matthew Little, (RM Museum); Simon Moody, (RAF Museum); John Morcombe; Mandy Nelson; Edward Perry; Séverine Peugniez, (Fampoux); the Platt Family, (Mrs Clarke); Olivier et Bernadette Pollet, (Gavrelle); Mike Scott, (Cambridge); Paul Reed; Tallett Family, (Pauline, Georgina and Samantha); Fernard Tandant, (Roeux); Robin Sterndale Bennett; Alan Wakefield, (RAF Museum); Helen Upfield; the Wellard Family, (Betty Cole); Paul Wilkinson; and Andrew Vollans.

If we have forgotten someone, please accept our apologies.

David Gruber in Sunken Road (1998), note shrapnel shells by sign.

7

PREFACE

Gavrelle is a small village on the Western Front in north east France. It was captured by the British in April 1917 during the battle of Arras. Gavrelle (and the rest of the eastern end of the Arras battlefield) are mainly neglected by history, lost between the battlefields of Ypres/Passendaele to the north and the Somme to the south, and overshadowed by the famous Vimy Ridge, a few kilometres to the northwest.

Some people think that because they have never heard of Gavrelle, that nothing much happened here. This is far from the truth, for Gavrelle was a great slaughter ground of the First World War, the stage of numerous battles and victories, and many hundreds of soldiers, sailors, airmen and civilians lost their lives here. We hope this book contributes to correcting this oversight by historians and visitors to the Western Front.

This guide is based around the monuments and cemeteries in and around Gavrelle. Many of the trenches, lost under modern agriculture, have also been mapped so that visitors can orientate themselves on the battlefield.

Both the authors have the Royal Naval Division as their main interest in Gavrelle; however, this volume has been widened to include as many actions over as long a time period as possible, and it is hoped that some sort of balance has been achieved. Even the battles in the skies above Gavrelle have been mentioned. The battle of 'Bloody April' of 1917 was fought over many villages in the Arras area, and Gavrelle was one of them.

Even though most of the guide is about Gavrelle during the Great War, the village was also a minor battlefield during the Second World War, the results of which added more war graves to the communes. Their story is briefly told.

The problem of defining boundaries for the guide has presented some difficulties. Beside the village itself, the fields around Gavrelle naturally saw much trench warfare, so the in-depth study of the guide covers the area within the commune boundaries.

Unfortunately most of the war graves in Gavrelle were moved out of the area after the Armistice to larger cemeteries. These are covered in the car tour of the cemeteries. This guide is the first to cover this area of the forgotten battlefields east of Arras/Vimy Ridge and if the authors have wandered slightly, it was to put Gavrelle into a wider

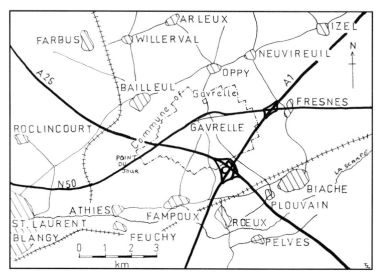

Map 1: The boundaries of the Commune of Gavrelle.

picture and as an introduction to the surrounding villages, most of which will be covered by future books in the *Battleground Europe* series.

We hope we have shown not only the traumatic history of this village in France, but also what there is to see, visit and discover in this part of the Western Front. Enjoy your visit to Gavrelle and remember all those who never returned home.

Trevor Tasker, Swansea, Wales. – Kyle Tallett, Ashford, Kent.

This book is dedicated to all those who lost their lives in and around Gavrelle during the twentieth century.

Mention should be made to Colin Fox, who died of cancer shortly after the guide on Monchy-les-Preux was published, and who did so much to promote the forgotten battlefields east of Arras, (south of the River Scarpe).

WHERE TO STAY

There are many places to stay the night in the immediate area; two hotels (with bath & T.V.), two camp sites and a Bed & Breakfast, which should cater for varied budgets.

The area has suffered from being visited just for a few hours, while passing through on the way to more popular battlefields such as the Somme. One of the aims of this guide is to show how much conflict there was in the region, and what can be seen and discovered, if only people took the time. An overnight stop in the area is recommended and even a few days stay should be contemplated.

Those travelling from Calais along the Autoroute A26, soon after passing the Canadian Memorial on Vimy Ridge, exit the autoroute at Thélus, driving through Thélus and Bailleul-sir-Berthoult, and then to Gavrelle. At the centre crossroads, turn left towards Douai and the HOTEL LE MANOIR is on your right. This is a two star hotel costing about 250F for the night. This hotel is the site of the strategic Mayor's House, which features in this guide. The hotel's garden was the Mayor's Garden during the war and staying in Le Manoir will give you access to the Mayor's Garden which marks the British Front Line of late 1917.

Those travelling along the A1 should exit at Fresnes-les-Montauban, where the Motel L'AQUARIUM is situated; here a room

Map 2: Where to stay, showing the location of two hotels, two camping sites, and Bed & Breakfast in the area.

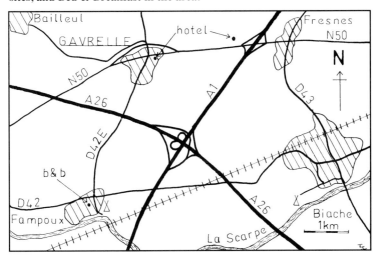

can be obtained for around 230F a night. This motel is only a short walk from the site of Gavrelle Windmill.

For those wishing to camp, Biache Municipal camping site is west of Biache; between the Scarpe canal and a lake. It costs about 40F per person for the night. There is also a supermarket in Biache. The camping at Fampoux is more expensive, about 50F a night; and there is no 'on site' office and payment must be made at the Mairie in the village.

The farm Bed and Breakfast (chambres d'hôtes) has five rooms on the top floor of a farmhouse, opposite the brewery in Fampoux. It costs about 140F (200F for two people) for the night, (continental breakfast included). Also included is a communal TV room with a fridge. Mme Peugniez speaks some English.

LE MANOIR Hotel, 35 Route Nationale, Gavrelle, (03.21.58.68.58) (http://www.cofrase.com/hotel/lemanoir)

L'AQUARIUM Motel, Route Nationale 50, Fresnes-Les-Montauban, (03.21.50.00.13)

CAMPING MUNICIPAL <<Les Etangs>> Commune de Biache-Saint-Vaast

CAMPING MUNICIPAL, Commune de Fampoux

CHAMBRES D'HOTES, 17 Rue Paul Verlaine, Fampoux, (03.21.55.00.90)

Aerial photograph of the area east of Gavrelle. In the foreground is L'Aqarium Motel where the TGV crosses the N50. The Gavrelle by-pass can be seen far left, with an 'x' marking the site of the Gavrelle Windmill. Oppy wood is in the background.

ADVICE TO VISITORS

Most guide books to the Front carry statutory warnings to beware battlefield debris and strongly urging people not to touch or take them away as souvenirs. This guide does not want to over emphasise the risks to the extent that the visitor is afraid to drive down a lane in case they hit a shell whilst turning around. The ploughed fields around Gavrelle today yield unexploded shells (including gas), and hand grenades and bullets, this is all evidence of the terrible conflict at Gavrelle. These battlefield ordnances are relatively safe IF LEFT ALONE. They do, even today, cause casualties, but most are from people who deliberately interfere with them.

In fact, statistically speaking, there is infinitely more danger from car accidents than any other danger, and care and caution should be taken, whether you are driving, cycling or walking the battlefield.

The area surrounding Gavrelle is a crossroads of Europe, which is why it has been a battlefield for all those centuries, being on the marching routes of invading and defending armies. Even today, two of

Ploughed up near the Windmill in the 1990s. A large and medium artillery shells, and two Stokes mortars. Note beer bottle for scale.

the main motorways in northern France cross just south of Gavrelle and the new high speed rail link runs through the area. This book is mainly about the slaughter in this area at the beginning of the century, but keep in mind the great danger at the end of the century (all over the world, not only in Gavrelle), of death rates on the roads, and caution is required in the Gavrelle area.

This guide also includes walks. We are aware that due to infirmity or weather conditions some may use their cars to cover the walks, but we strongly advise visitors to walk whenever possible. The area is relatively flat, but only when walking are you aware of the fields of fire of the battlefield and the small dips in the landscape that could hide a whole battalion from view.

All the walks are off the fast main roads, but care must also be taken on the country roads. Always walk on the left facing the traffic. We live in an age where motorists think that they are the only people who use these roads. Not only are cars a danger on the roads and lanes, they also can be a danger 'off the road' as well. In the early 1990's a car coming from Fampoux crashed through the south wall of Chili Trench Cemetery, demolishing many headstones in the cemetery. In the autumn of 1997 a car came off the N50, just missed the RND Anchor Monument, and demolished one of the flagpoles. (Which is why the two flagpoles are slightly different.)

The car tour of the ten cemeteries takes four to five hours; if you try to do it in under three hours, you may kill yourself on the roads, and also take someone 'walking the battlefields' with you. The more time you take visiting the area, the more you will appreciate the battlefield, and the safer you will be.

In early 2000 the access road to the RND memorial was separated from those exiting the N50. It is no longer to do as shown below, where a car exiting the N50 is accelerating to overtake two cars when only a few seconds away from a Primary School.

THE MAPS

List of maps:

15

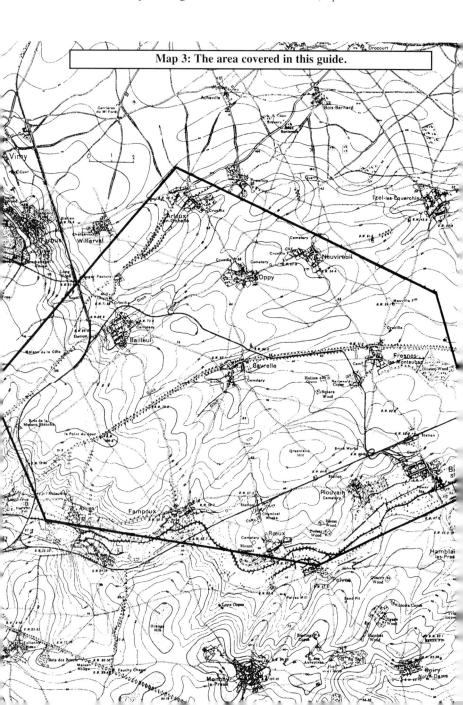

Map 3: The area covered in this guide.

Chapter One

INTRODUCTION

Gavrelle is not a battlefield park. It is a village and commune in northern France on the old Western Front. Its scars of war have been mostly healed by the rebuilding of the village after its total destruction in 1917 and the wasteland of trenches has been returned to cultivated fields. Modern agricultural practices, and fast communication routes that criss-cross the region, have altered the landscape and hidden or disguised the haunted acres of the battlefield. This chapter is an introduction to the area and an attempt to reconstruct a historical landscape, lost but not forgotten.

The village of Gavrelle contains a population of nearly 400, which is slightly larger than during the Great War. One advantage of its communication links is that this small village has three cafes and a two star hotel. It is still basically an agricultural village and has twelve farms, which work the land in the commune that has not been swallowed up by the motorways, dual carriageway and *TGV* high speed train.

Gavrelle lies on a fertile plain, surrounded by the towns of Arras, Lens and Douai. The British and Canadians called the area the Douai Plain, because they were always attacking in the direction of Douai, but the French call it the Lens Plain, as it is in Pas de Calais while Douai is in the neighbouring department of the Nord. This patch of fertile land supplied food for the factory workers and miners of the surrounding area. It is a strange mixture of rural and urban, with agricultural and industrial side by side. Emile Zola set his novel *Germinal* on this coalfield in northern France. The book opens with a description of a mine and small workers' cottages by night. The hero *Etienne* crosses a sugar beet field en route to the mine to ask for work.[1]

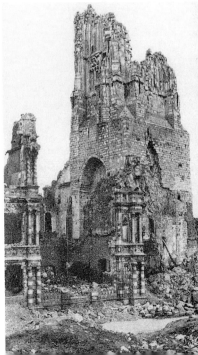

The Belfrey at Arras.

If it were possible to obtain a pigeon's eye view from the top of the church steeple of Gavrelle, the Belfry at Arras would be seen. The wooded rise of Vimy Ridge can be seen on the western horizon. To the

17

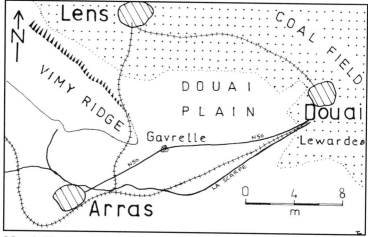

Map 4: The Douai Plain and surrounding area.

north and north east lie the slag heaps from the Lens and Douai coalfields. Coal production, in decline since the 1960s, has stopped altogether and the pit winding gears are disappearing from the skyline. At least one of the slag heaps has been converted into a dry ski-slope. The Renault Car Factory east of Douai now marks where Richthofen's Jasta 11, (his 'flying circus'), was based. Behind this is the Belfry of Douai, painted by Camille Corot[2] in 1871, just after the Franco-Prussian War, when conquering German troops marched through the area. At Lewarde,[3] south of Douai, one of the mines has been preserved in a museum. To the south the river Scarpe, deep in the Scarpe valley, cannot be seen, but the church steeples of Roeux, Biache, Vitry, Brebieres and Courchelettes mark the canalised Scarpe which connects Arras and Douai.

The area was originally populated by a Celtic tribe, the Atrebates. There was a Roman settlement at Arras with Roman roads radiating outwards, one of which connected Arras to Tourcoing. Along this route were many villages, including Gavrelle, which through the centuries became a convenient staging post, with an inn and stables to change horses. Just after the first millennium a small priory, a satellite of St Vaast Abbey in Arras, was established in Gavrelle. When this went into decline the buildings and ruins were used as farm buildings. Just after the French Revolution in 1797, an 'observation post' was set up in Gavrelle, garrisoned by cavalry. Even today horses are a part of the village, with stables and recently built equestrian accessory shop.

This northern area of France has been described by British visitors as being flat and boring, but some French artists took the opposite view. Corot had a summer studio at Arras and painted the landscape of the area. One of his paintings, in the Louvre in Paris, is a tree lined road with cottages at Sin-en-Noble, (now a suburb of Douai). Aerial photographs taken by the Royal Flying Corps during the Great War show the long shadows of the tall poplars which lined the Arras to Douai road.

The Great War broke out when the Germans invaded Belgium and France. The Schlieffen Plan was designed to thrust through the Lille and Arras area, and attack Paris from behind. Modifications to the plan resulted in a swing south, where the invaders were stopped at the river Marne. While the Battle of the Marne was in progress German cavalry entered Arras on 6 September 1914 but were driven out three days later. When the Battle of the Marne ended on 9 September both sides tried to outflank each other, resulting in a string of battles to the north, misleadingly referred to as 'the Race to the Sea'. In October the fighting reached the Arras area. On 1 October 1914 the Germans arrived in Douai, forcing out a small French garrison, and British armoured cars of the Royal Naval Air Service.[4] The Germans pushed west towards Arras and Lens.

French grave in Point-du-jour Cemetery, west of Gavrelle.

French divisions were transferred from the quieter fronts in the south, some were transported to Arras, and rushed east to meet the Germans. Early on the morning of 2 October, along a line Méricourt, Fresnoy, Oppy, Gavrelle, Roeux and Monchy the French and Germans clashed. Many French soldiers died in an attempt to push the Germans back, just west of Gavrelle.[5] At Gavrelle a scouting party of French Dragoons confronted the Germans. A

French troops on the way to the front. Taylor Library

German photograph of the Windmill and out-houses. This photograph is taken from the Gavrelle-Izel lane, along which the 23rd French Dragoons were advancing, when they were fired upon from the window of the Windmill. The hole just below the window is shell damage from the 2 October 1914 fighting.

German machine-gun, sited in a window of the windmill, killed twelve, including the young officer, sous-lieutenant Grabias de Bagneris. The French were slowly pushed back and Lens was captured on 4 October. Vimy Ridge was also taken but Arras stubbornly resisted, in spite of being heavily bombarded. Once again stalemate set in and both sides tried to outflank to the north.

The British Expeditionary Force came from the Marne, detrained and fought north of Lens. This front was held and the battles moved to Belgium, and eventfully to the sand dunes of the Belgian coast.

General Joffre resumed the fighting in the Arras area, but 1914 ended in the Artois mud of a rainy December. General Joffre, writing in his journal at the end of 1914, shows the French position and their determination to win an offensive victory in 1915.

> *My intention of enveloping the German right had not been entirely realised. We had merely succeeded in retaining (in itself no small result) the French Coast of the English Channel, a narrow strip of Belgian territory and part of our northern coal field basin. On the other hand, we had lost Lens and the valuable centres of Lille, Roubaix and Tourcoing, whilst the Germans still held on to Noyon, less than 65 miles from Paris.*
>
> *The best and largest portion of the German army was on our soil, with its line of battle jutting out a mere five days march from the heart of France. This situation made clear to every Frenchman that our task consisted in defeating the enemy, and driving him out of our country.*[6]

In 1914 General Joffre had to order rationing of artillery shells. In 1915 he thought enough

RFC photograph of Abbey Farm, April 1917. The ruins of the Abbey church can be seen, and the square of the old cloister, with dovecote and pond.

Aerial photograph, 1998, of the site of Abbey Farm. The church was rebuilt roughly in the same place.

ammunition would be available to smash the front and break through. The axis point was Lens, with the French attacking Notre Dame de Lorette and Vimy Ridge and the British north of Lens. Two major offensives of May and September gained little ground but made Vimy Ridge quite vulnerable. The Germans were concerned about the constant pressure on their line in this area and built a strong system of three defensive lines, the third line running just west of Gavrelle. Along this line were observation balloons which observed the Front at Vimy Ridge and another strongpoint known as 'The Labyrinth', only 12 kilometres from Gavrelle. Greenland Hill, south of Gavrelle, was also known as Balloon Hill.[7]

One of the German soldiers in this region was a young art student from Dresden, Otto Dix.[8] This machine gunner sketched the trenches of Vimy Ridge and scenes of life behind the lines in the Lens and Méricourt area.

Another German soldier who fought here, and known to have been billeted in Gavrelle, was Alfons Schneider. Schneider wrote about life with the villagers of Gavrelle, with the women of the village doing the battalion's laundry. There was an observation balloon near the Windmill, with an artillery battery sheltering in the dip behind it. Schneider wrote about an estaminent halfway between Gavrelle and Point-du-Jour, probably the site of 'Lonely House'. This abandoned estaminent was reinforced with concrete and hid a 77mm gun. This position was never bothered by enemy artillery and Schneider speculated that the French never knew of its existence. However, the

German occupation photograph postcard of Rue de Roeux, looking north. On the right is the blacksmith and a German monument made out of used artillery shells.

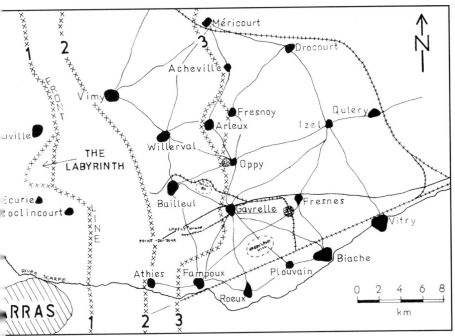

Map 5: German three lines of defence north-east of Arras.

rats also exploited this secluded spot and used to slide down the roof as if in some tobogganing game.[9] When off-duty Schneider would take one of the thoroughbred horses at Gavrelle and tour the occupied villages in the area. Many dugouts were made at Gavrelle and an elaborate tunnelling system planned, but a ventilation problem developed and the vast tunnel system at nearby Roeux could not be repeated at Gavrelle.

German Occupation twin photograph post card of Gavrelle, showing the Church, used by the Germans as a hospital, and the heavy traffic outside. There are no leaves on the trees, so the photograph was probably taken in the winter of 1914/1915.

As the occupation of Gavrelle went from months to years, a distinctive Germanic flavour changed Gavrelle. A German monument of artillery shells was built in the village. The church became a military hospital, and the Gavrelle to Douai road saw the constant traffic of supply wagons and ambulances. In 1915 a German cemetery was made

Plan of Gavrelle 1916, with German occupation postcards showing the Germanic presence. Capron Family Collection

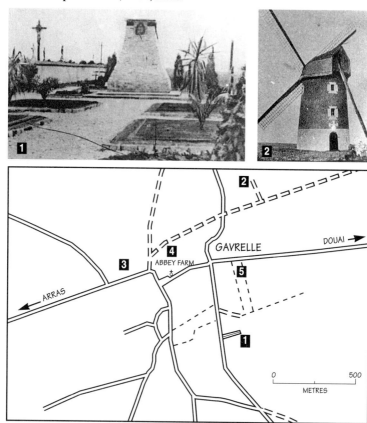

south of the village cemetery (which over time became larger than the village cemetery) to take the casualties who died at the Front or at Gavrelle before they could be evacuated to the main hospital at Douai.

In early 1916 the Germans went on the offensive and attacked Verdun. French troops in the Arras/Lens area were needed at Verdun and in the March the British took over the line. 1916 is notable for the Battle of the Somme, as well as Verdun, but fighting also occurred at

DOVECOTE

DOVECOTE

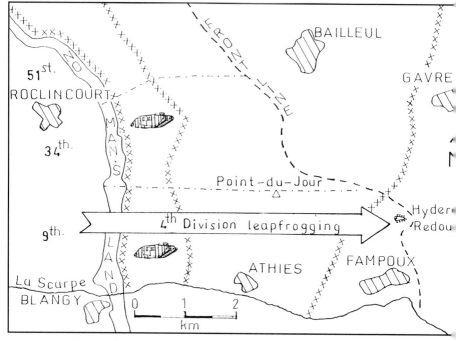

Map 6: The attack area of XVII Corps, 9 April 1917.

Vimy Ridge, including a major but limited attack by the Germans in May 1916.

All the offensives of 1915 and 1916 altered the Front Line very little, all that seemed to result was an increase in the size of the numerous military cemeteries in the area, including the German cemetery at Gavrelle. At the end of 1916 General Joffre was replaced by General Nivelle, an artillery officer who had made a reputation with his success at the end of the long Verdun Battle. Nivelle planned a new offensive to win the war in 1917. This offensive would include his allies at Arras in a diversionary attack.

The winter of 1916/1917 was the coldest for decades, creating great hardship in the trenches and behind the lines. In the occupied villages the houses were stripped for firewood, even staircases were chopped up and replaced by ladders. The Germans constructed a fourth defensive line: the Drocourt-Quéant Line, which ran a few kilometres east of Gavrelle. Because of the Royal Navy blockade of Germany, there were acute shortages of food and materials. The French population of the occupied areas were now regarded as extra mouths to feed and by March 1917 most of the villagers of Gavrelle were sent to un-occupied

France via Switzerland.

Even by early April signs of spring had not yet arrived. If the cold was deadly in the trenches, it was worse above the trenches, in an open cockpit. Lieutenant Peter Warren RFC, (one of Manfred von Richthofen's victims), explains the extreme weather conditions on 2 April 1917, the day he was shot down over Vimy Ridge.

> We left the aerodrome at 10:30 in the morning. The weather was bad - rain and hail, with almost a gale blowing in the direction of the German lines. Our faces were covered with whale oil to prevent frost-bite. So many flyers had been laid up with frost-bitten faces that the use of the grease was compulsory, and a case of frost-bite became an offence calling for a court martial.[10]

The Battle of Arras started on Easter Monday 9 April 1917, after a week long bombardment. The weather was still wintery, with a bitter westerly wind and snow flurries. The Canadians were to take Vimy Ridge, whilst the gap between the Ridge and the Scarpe was the task of XVII Corps, with the 51st (Highland) Division in the north, then the 34th Division, and then the 9th (Scottish) Division. Both the 9th and 34th were allotted four tanks each, but these were soon knocked out by German artillery or broke down. Once the Front Line was taken the 4th Division was sent 'leapfrogging' through, to push the line back further and capture more ground before any counter-attacks could be organised.

Accounts of the first day of the Battle of Arras are often dominated by the Canadian Corps which captured Vimy Ridge, but XVII Corps advanced to the German third line of defence and captured a strongpoint known as Hyderabad Redoubt, south of Gavrelle. This was a distance of five kilometres – three and a half miles – and, as the Official History states, it was the longest advance in a single day since trench warfare had started in 1914.[11] The advance was so rapid that a German general was captured when walking along the Fampoux-Gavrelle road after being deserted by his chauffeur.

The battalion of the 4th Division responsible for capturing Hyderabad Redoubt was 1/Rifle Brigade. The Battalion War Diary describes the action.

> On approaching HYDERABAD Redoubt it was seen that the wire surrounding it was entirely unbroken and on the Western Face there were only two gaps in the wire. This necessitated a further closing in of the men to get into the Redoubt. Fortunately there was very little opposition and the Redoubt was easily

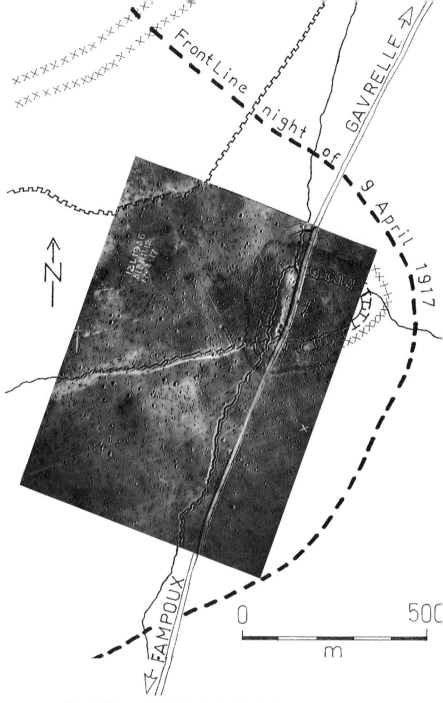

Map 7: The capture of Hyderabad Redoubt, 9 April 1917. The complex defences of this redoubt can be seen, including the surrounding belt of wire. The aerial photograph (IWM) was taken 17 April 1917. The Fampoux-Gavrelle road is clearly shown. It was on this road, on 9 April 1917, that a German General was captured, after being deserted by his chauffeur.

occupied, Number 11 Platoon drop-kicking a football into the Redoubt and rushing in after it.

The Third Company ("B") had been dropped at the SUNKEN ROAD and quickly cleared the dugouts there and occupied HYMEN and HALO Trenches, east of the road.

The two leading companies ("C" and "A") were only able to enter the Redoubt by two entrances and there was a good deal of confusion at first; and re-organisation was rendered more difficult by the great depth and narrowness of the trenches. Consolidation was, however, started as soon as possible in small groups to clear the Redoubt, and outpost and patrols were sent out. These, however, and all parties outside the Redoubt, were heavily fired on and sniped at by the enemy who were lying out in the open between the Redoubt and the Gavrelle-Roeux road and came under Machine Gun fire from the North and East. The Patrol could not make headway and as the Consolidation Parties were being picked off one by one the officer in charge at the Redoubt withdrew them and occupied and consolidated the "T" heads, blocks being established in the communication trenches running North and East from the Redoubt. By this time it was getting dark and the Redoubt was being heavily shelled.[12]

Colonel-General Freiherr von Falkenhausen, commanding the Sixth German Army in the area, was criticised by his superiors for being too elastic in his defence, most of his divisions were near Douai. Falkenhausen had mis-calculated the attack on his front, he had expected the attack around mid-April, the same time as the expected French attack to the south. He had withdrawn many of his divisions to Douai out of range of the artillery. The Canadians and British had broken through to the third line of defence, and the strategically important Vimy Ridge had been captured.

After years of being several kilometres behind the Front, Gavrelle was now the German Front Line. Plans were made for a new offensive to push the Front Line further east, which would include the capture of Gavrelle. The weather was finally starting to change and spring was in the air. The Germans also had time to bring up their fresh divisions from Douai.

The actions from 9-14 April 1917 are known as the First Battle of the Scarpe. Another attack was planned for the 23 April, to be known as the Second Battle of the Scarpe.

Most of the villagers had been repatriated, but a handful had stayed behind. One was Victorine Capron, the miller's wife. She was killed

Victorine Capron, the miller's wife, killed by a British shell, in the preliminary bombardment of Gavrelle, a few days before the capture of Gavrelle. She was one of two civilian victims of Gavrelle in the Great War.

when the village was shelled in the preliminary bombardment, before the 23 April attack and capture of Gavrelle.

1. Emile Zola (1840-1902) did his research for *Germinal* in a mining village near Valenciennes, part of the same coalfield. *Germinal* was published in 1885.

2. Camille Corot, (1796-1875), French painter known for his landscapes which were a mixture of classical, romantic and natural. It is said he influenced the Impressionists.

3. Centre historique miniere at Lewarde. Situated just south east of Douai, it is an old colliery converted into a working show museum.

4. A squadron of Royal Naval Air Service armoured cars landed at Dunkerque in August 1914. They were used to protect RNAS aerodromes, but ranged far and wide, engaging enemy patrols in many skirmishes.

5. In May 1917, a stretcher bearer, Joseph Yarwood, was just west of Gavrelle when he noticed red rags flapping in the wind. On closer inspection he found them to be the bones and rags from uniforms of about thirty French soldiers from 1914. (IWM Sound Archive, A/12231/12).

6. *My Memoirs*, by Marshal Joffre, (1932), translated by T. Bentley Mott.

7. *Cheerful Sacrifice*, (1990), by Jonathan Nicholls.

8. The painter Otto Dix, (1891-1969) was a machine gunner in the Lens area during 1915, and drew many sketches of the neighbourhood. His nightmarish vision was a vivid comment on contemporary society during and after the war.

9. *Dans la trenchee devant Arras*, by Alfons Schneider, a German who fought in the area and was billeted at Gavrelle. In 1997 his book was published in French; Schneider promoted the book one Sunday in the community centre at Gavrelle.

10. *The Red Knight of Germany*, (1927), by Floyd Gibbons.

11. *Military Operations, France and Belgium 1917*, Vol. I, (1947), by Cyril Falls.

12. War Diary of the 1/Rifle Brigade, (PRO WO95/1496).

Chapter Two

CAPTURE, 23 APRIL 1917

The Battle of Arras opened on 9 April 1917. At the start of this offensive Gavrelle lay some miles behind the lines, but by the second week of the offensive it was to see fighting. Gavrelle was important because it was part of the Arleux Loop, a defensive line of significant importance. The Germans wanted to hold the allied armies on this line

Map 8: German defences from the Arleux Loop to Hyderabad Redout.

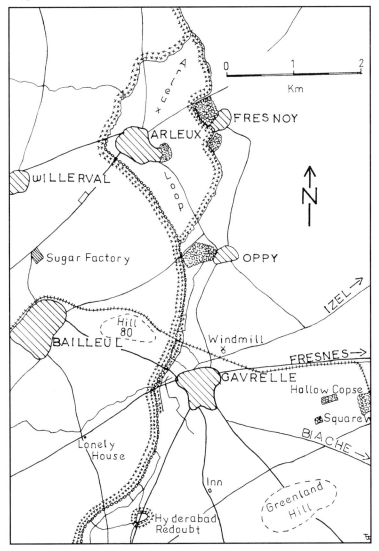

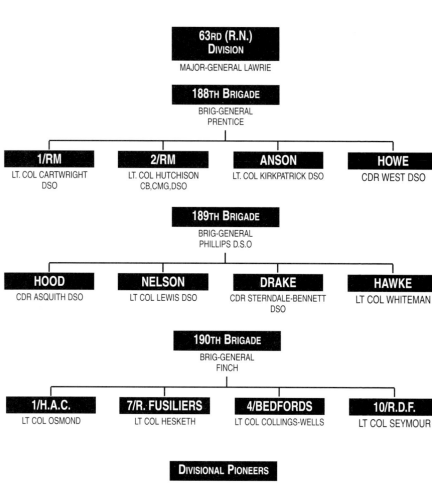

63RD (R.N.) DIVISION

MAJOR-GENERAL LAWRIE

188TH BRIGADE

BRIG-GENERAL
PRENTICE

1/RM	**2/RM**	**ANSON**	**HOWE**
LT. COL CARTWRIGHT DSO	LT. COL HUTCHISON CB,CMG,DSO	LT. COL KIRKPATRICK DSO	CDR WEST DSO

189TH BRIGADE

BRIG-GENERAL
PHILLIPS D.S.O

HOOD	**NELSON**	**DRAKE**	**HAWKE**
CDR ASQUITH DSO	LT COL LEWIS DSO	CDR STERNDALE-BENNETT DSO	LT COL WHITEMAN

190TH BRIGADE

BRIG-GENERAL
FINCH

1/H.A.C.	**7/R. FUSILIERS**	**4/BEDFORDS**	**10/R.D.F.**
LT COL OSMOND	LT COL HESKETH	LT COL COLLINGS-WELLS	LT COL SEYMOUR

DIVISIONAL PIONEERS

14/Worcester

The Order of Battle of 63rd (RN) Division as of April 1917.

whilst their half-finished defences behind were completed. If Gavrelle and the high ground to the north of the village could be taken, then the British army would have excellent observation of practically the whole Douai plain, and perhaps breakout on to it. The task of taking this ground to the north of it fell to the 63rd (RN) Division. The capture of Gavrelle was an important part of this unique Division's history.

On the opening day of the offensive the RND was split up, the divisional artillery supporting the Canadians' assault of Vimy Ridge whilst the individual battalions were attached to assaulting divisions. The RND was pulled together again after a few days, and on 14 April it moved into the line west of Gavrelle with 189 and 190 Brigades in the front line. The brigades were slightly separated due to the fact that 190 Brigade's position was to the rear of 189 and it needed to be brought forward. This was first attempted on the 15th, in broad daylight, by 10/Royal Dublin Fusiliers and 4/Bedfords, but the attempt failed with severe losses. This was tried again during the night of 16th/17th by 7/Royal Fusiliers and 1/Honorable Artillery Company and this time succeeded in advancing the line, which they then consolidated. The front line was now on the forward slope of the Point du Jour ridge, which meant that the Germans to the east in Gavrelle had excellent observation into the British front line trenches. This made basic living conditions difficult; getting supplies, relief and just moving were done under German observation and interference. The reserve trenches lay along the Point du Jour ridge and behind it. This was the German front line on 9 April; now it has the 9th Division memorial on it. If you stand here you can see the dip in the land downwards unfortunately the motorway ruins the view! The weather was cold, it was sleeting and snowing, and the trenches were in bad repair. Gavrelle lay ahead, a fortified village in the German 3rd line of the forward Hindenburg defences. The ground between was clear, flat and untouched, unlike the moonscape that the troops were used to. Joe Murray of the Hood:

> *The ground in front of us, in front of Gavrelle, wasn't pock marked with shell holes like on the Somme or Ancre. It was quite level really, open, ideal territory for tanks, but we didn't have any! Open was all right as we could more or less go forward in a line, rather than dodge through shell holes.*[1]

The French Nivelle offensive to the south had now failed and German eyes were concentrated on the British and their intentions. Patrols reported that the Germans held their front line strongly and gave every intention of holding their line. The RND position was a bad one and did not offer good long-term prospects. As the Divisional History (by Douglas Jerrold) put it, they had to get on or get out. It was decided to get on. The move was to be made on 23 April, St George's Day, in conjunction with 37th Division on the southern boundary.

The attack was to be made by units of 190 and 189 Brigade. The task of 190 Brigade was as follows: 7/Royal Fusiliers and 4/Bedfords were to take the German front line to the north of 189 Brigade, to form a defensive flank for 189 Brigade as they advanced. They were to secure the high ground on the left of the village including the windmill, which would allow189 to advance unmolested; 1/HAC were to act as support if needed. The task of 189 Brigade was hard, it involved the taking of Gavrelle itself. The objectives, for a change, would be readily identifiable on the ground, as they were roads in a village that was still standing. 189 Brigade's objectives were as follows: Nelson and Drake were to attack the village with the Arras-Fresnes road forming the inter-battalion boundary, Hood battalion would follow behind in support. The first objective (Blue Line) was the German front line, which was just outside the village. The second objective (Yellow Line) was the road, which ran from Gavrelle southwards, perpendicular to the line of advance. This was easily identifiable and would enable the attacking battalions to orientate themselves before going onto the third objective, Green Line, which was the German trench line 350 yards east of Gavrelle. This would link up with 37th Division, whose final objective was to take Greenland Hill, a dominating feature to the south east of Gavrelle. The remaining battalions of 189 and 190 Brigades, 10/RDF and Hawke Battalion, were to be used as carrying parties. Howe Battalion was put on standby to help, as was the rest of 188

Map 9: RND plan of attack on Gavrelle, showing the Brigade boundaries and objectives, 23 April 1917. (PRO)

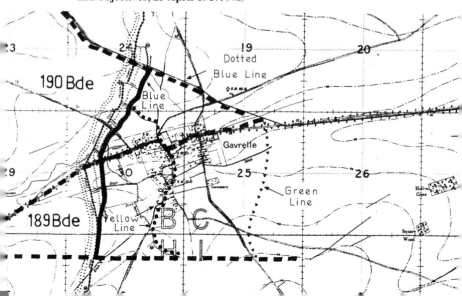

Brigade, which was in divisional reserve.

On 20 April Lt.Col Freyberg VC, Commanding Officer of the Hood Battalion[2], was appointed Brigadier-General in the 58th Division with immediate effect. This was a blow as it meant that Hood were left without a familiar commander on the eve of battle, but the problem was overcome by the appointment of Commander Arthur Asquith as his successor. Asquith was no stranger to the Hood, he was an original officer of theirs from Gallipoli times and served with them on the Somme, after which he had been assigned to intelligence duties. As he was the former Prime Minister's son, he had been kept out of the line for some time, especially after the loss of his brother, Raymond[3], but he was the type of man who tried every trick to get as close to the action as possible. On hearing the Hood was leaderless, he contrived to rejoin the Hood. Permission was granted, and this very able officer rejoined his old unit on 21 April. Asquith was to make a terrific personal impact in the days ahead.

Lt Col Freyburg VC.

On 22 April reconnaissance patrols were sent out and aerial missions were undertaken. The latter was done at great personal risk as this was a period known as 'Bloody April', the RFC were being shot out of the skies, and over Gavrelle the von Richtofen 'Flying Circus' was dominant. Aerial photographs and patrols revealed the wire well cut in front of Gavrelle, but on the southern part of the Drake

Commander Arthur Asquith.

sector it was still strong. This caused some degree of concern and Brigadier Phillips asked if the attack should still go ahead. The answer was yes; but Commander Sterndale-Bennett, the Commanding Officer of Drake, was asked to modify his attack plan. It was decided that instead of attacking on a two-company front, the two right hand companies would form up behind the left-hand companies and go through the wire that was cut and once through, then fan out to the right. Additional mortars and machine guns were put on the right to make up for this narrow frontage.

Commander Sterndale-Bennett was another exceptional leader. He was one of the youngest battalion commanders in the BEF, at just 23. His potential was spotted during the Battle of the Ancre. When the senior officers of his battalion were killed or wounded early in the battle, he re-organised and led his men onto success. He was awarded the DSO for this, promoted to Commander and put in command of

German machine gun team in action.

Drake. The high calibre of commanding officers of the assaulting battalions was to play a major part in the success.

On the morning of 23 April at 4.45am the assault commenced. Nelson and Drake were through the wire and took the first objective within ten minutes. The battalions became badly disorganised going through the wire, but the casualties were relatively light except for D Company of the Drake, which was badly shot up in this process. Hood battalion had been ordered to wait until the first objective had been taken and the barrage moved on. Asquith knew that when the attack started the Germans would shell the British assembly trenches, with the likely result of the death of many of his battalion. He chose to ignore this command and as soon as the Nelson got going he personally led his men forward. Joe Murray describes it:

> *The instruction was that we were not to move until the barrage had lifted off the German front line. Anyone knows to wait until the barrage lifts and walk 400 yards would be murder. Asquith, instead of waiting till the barrage lifted, took us forward to about within 50 yards of the barrage, and we*

Leading Seaman Joseph Murray.

were on top of his line before Jerry knew anything about it. We men of the Hood who survived the battle owe our survival to Asquith.[4]

The German front line trenches had been taken and the assaulting forces consolidated by clearing out the support lines, a process described by Sterndale-Bennett:

Zero Hour, Barrage opened and men moved forward in fine style. Zero hour plus 3 mins Enemy wire encountered, this wire was terrifically thick and the leading waves became immediately disorganised in their endeavours to find gaps. I then thought it essential to leave H.Q. and try and straighten things out. We managed to get them all through the wire and at Zero + 8Mins we assaulted the German front line with great success. B Coy (the second Coy in the original formation) worked down to the right flank and got rid of any Germans that were causing trouble. The leading Coy (D Coy) suffered very badly going through the wire from enemy rifle and MG fire and all their officers, except the Coy Commander (Sub Lt Wallis) became casualties. Gave orders to C. Coy (3rd wave) to keep in touch with Kings Royal Rifle Corps at all costs, which they did very well. Mopping up continued until Zero +12mins, then went for the German support line. We met with little opposition with the exception of small enemy parties, which were soon dispersed. The advance continued under excellent leadership by the officers and NCOs and the way that the men kept close to the barrage absolutely fearlessly was truly magnificent.[5]

With the first objective taken, the advance continued onto the second objective in the village, which was taken within forty minutes of the start of the advance. Drake was just to the south of the village, Hood with Nelson was just inside the village. The fighting in the village was a bit confusing. There were numerous short-range engagements, which Asquith describes thus:

We advanced again slowly and half right through the village to the Yellow Line. The enemy were still sniping at our men from cottages. They were fired at by our men and rushed, and a good deal of mixed fighting at 20 yards range took place. The enemy were still sending up red rain rockets from these cottages, which some of the Nelson and our men had passed. A few of our guns were still firing short and were causing casualties among our own men.[6]

Joe Murray was also in the thick of it:

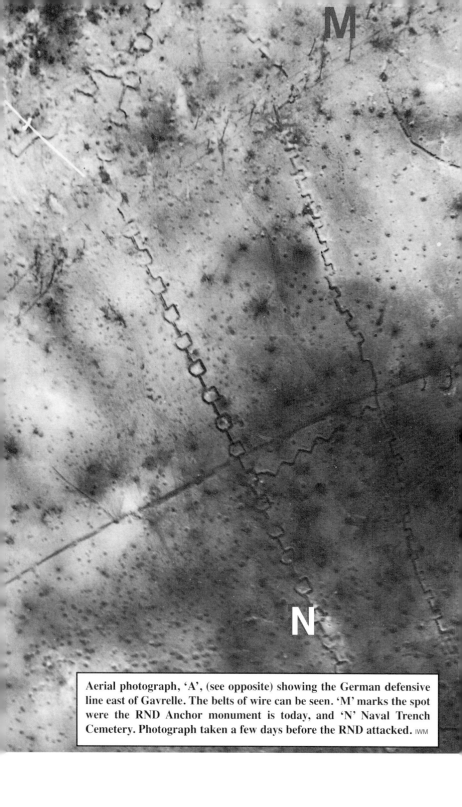

M

N

Aerial photograph, 'A', (see opposite) showing the German defensive line east of Gavrelle. The belts of wire can be seen. 'M' marks the spot were the RND Anchor monument is today, and 'N' Naval Trench Cemetery. Photograph taken a few days before the RND attacked. IWM

When we got into the village it was different. Jerries were in the cellars and we were in the open, and by then it was quite light, so we were perfect targets. In the village there were bricks flying about, rifle and machine-gun fire. You couldn't keep in any formation. Sometimes you got under a half blown-down house, and other times you got over the top. The wire in front was piled up in heaps, as it usually was by an artillery bombardment. We had to keep gathering together to get past a particular place. However, you could not climb over the 10-15 feet of bricks that had formed.

I remember as we got to the first objective it didn't seem too bad. We seemed to be organised, but when we got to the second objective, a road that runs through the village, oh, dear me! There was no line and no sort of direction. You couldn't see any officers and you couldn't see any men. Sometimes there were three or four together, and sometimes you were on your own, wondering where everybody had got to. When I got into this trench, which was just in front of a road, about 10-15 yards from it, I came across an officer lying down. He was lying flat and I remember trying to undo some barbed wire on what was left of one of his legs. He was a Sub-Lieutenant. I also remember turning him over and there was a sort of a grin on his face, which was red because of the brick dust, as well as the blood. Because of the smoke and dust, you had to spit all the time, you just couldn't help it, and you also kept rubbing your eyes.[7]

The advance had to stop here, as there was a planned hold in the

Map 10: Trench map of Gavrelle showing location of aerial photographs.

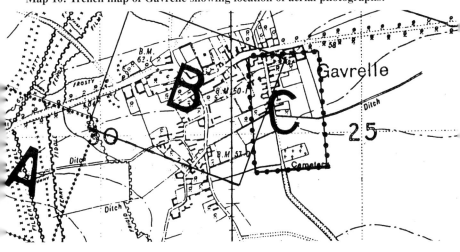

39

Aerial photograph 'B'(map 10). Abbey Farm can be seen middle top. The road running north south was the yellow line. Photograph taken a few days before the RND attacked. IWM

barrage to allow reorganisation before moving on. This worked against the RND, who probably could have gone on and pushed through the rest of the village, this break gave the Germans time to improve their defence and call down the artillery. Re-organisation was nearly

Aerial photograph of Gavrelle showing the 'yellow line'. (1998)

OPPY

YELLOW LINE

← TO RND MONUMENT

TO NAVAL TRENCH CEMETERY

FAMPOUX

impossible in the village, as there were two lots of artillery crashing down. Debris, smoke and dust was everywhere and the units were very mixed up. Drake were fortunate, just outside the village, in open country and thus it was easier to deploy, but Hood were mixed up with Nelson, and there were many Bedfords amongst them as well. Asquith noted in his diary:

> *At 5 .40am at the Yellow Line we reorganised. The street was crowded with Nelsons and Hoods in addition to about 100 Bedfords of the 190th Brigade, who should have been north of the main Arras-Fresnes road, defending our left flank. I collected their three officers and asked them to move north of the road, so as to defend our flank. I warned all I could that the barrage does not move forward till 6.01am. This pause of 20 minutes is a great mistake, giving the enemy a breathing space just when we have them on the run.*[8]

The above mentioned conversation between the Bedford's Commanding Officer, Lieutenant Colonel Collings-Wells and Asquith is a significant one. Collings-Wells won the VC just under a year later[9], Asquith, according to his men won the VC many times, and along with Sterndale-Bennett was recommended for one after

Lieutenant-Colonel J S Collings-Wells VC.

Map 11: Street plan of Gavrelle showing the Drake Battalion's attack, south of Gavrelle. The cross marks the original site of the grave of Chief Petty Officer Webster, Drake Battalion, who is now in Brown's Copse Cemetery.

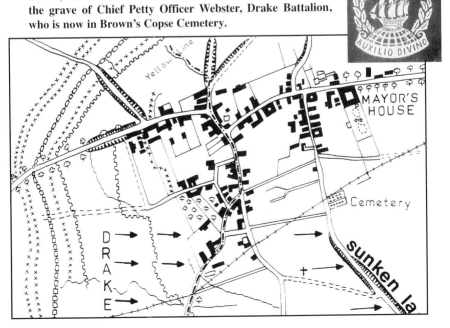

Gavrelle. It has often been said that being the ex-Prime Minister's son was the reason why he was never awarded this country's highest military honour.

The barrage moved forward, and the advance continued. For Hood the first 250 yards to the last objective involved travelling through the rest of the village; for Drake the country was open except for a walled civilian and German military cemetery to the front. Commander Sterndale-Bennett describes the Drake's remaining part of the day's action:

The Yellow line was captured at about zero +40mins. We had an excellent view of the village now and our left flank was engaging enemy machine guns and rifles which were firing from the southern outskirts of the village. The Lewis guns constantly came into action against enemy parties that were making a stand and were very effective. During this wait on the Yellow Line enemy snipers were quite active and Sub Lt. Wallis was hit through the head. The advance continued and wherever the enemy showed fight, our men made immediate dashes at him and put him out of

Photograph of Commander Walter Sterndale Bennett, and the last page of his journal on the capture of Gavrelle. He commanded the Drake Battalion and attacked southern Gavrelle as far as the Sunken Lane. He was later mortally wounded near Passchendaele in November 1917, and is buried in Dozinghem Military Cemetery, Belgium.

action or (in a few cases) sent him back as prisoners. The men's blood was up and few prisoners were taken. Owing to our having suffered pretty badly in the enemy's wire the men had little mercy. In the SUNKEN ROAD there was a considerable enemy garrison. They started to bolt but about 400 of them were reorganised under an officer and at one period it looked rather as if they were going to hold up the KRRs (who were not close enough to the barrage). Our advanced parties were ordered to rush up to the SUNKEN ROAD and attack the garrison on their right flank. They did this in excellent style bringing up a Lewis gun and enfilading the road. Those of the enemy that were left gave themselves up and had to run the gauntlet through our men as they ran back to the rear. The same Lewis gun took up a position on the eastern side of the road and played on the remainder of the garrison which was doubling towards SQUARE WOOD. Word was sent to the KRRs that their position was taken and they could come up when they thought fit. When the remainder of the Battalion came up we immediately pushed out our Lewis guns on to the high ground to the east of the road and gave our men a short rest. During this period many more of the enemy were cleared out of the small shelters in the SUNKEN ROAD and enemy tools were collected. I then went out to site my trenches. Expected to see the Nelson Battalion coming out of the village on my left but they did not show up. So I decided to dig my line using an enemy communication trench for my general alignment, keeping the men as much as possible off the road, and started to dig in. I saw a small party of the Nelson Battalion digging in about C.25.a. 6.1 So I decided to make towards this on my left flank and the cross roads C.25 c.9. 1. I decided this was my right flank as I was here in touch with 2 Companies of the KRRs. I had a splendid view of the valley ahead to FRESNES les MONTAUBAN and I felt that, as my flanks were doubtful, I could not do better than dig in where I was. The enemy machine guns's from about C 19 d 3.3 and C. 19 d 9.4 were giving us a lively time but we managed to rush out to shell holes on our right flank to the east of the road and the consolidation went on very successfully. The enemy then started to shell the road with 5.9's and I sent back for retaliation on Fresnes les Montauban on the OPPY gun line. The enemy during our consolidation were coming back in small parties and occupying trenches in the valley and some small areas of dead ground about 300 yards *from our position. I received no fire except for occasional sniping owing to the lack of SAA. During the afternoon a very formidable body of the enemy started to advance towards us in waves on a line stretching from about C.20 central to SQUARE WOOD. The number must have amounted to two brigades. I sent back immediately for the barrage to reopen. This was done and the enemy became thoroughly disorganised and on the left flank they started to retire along the road. However small parties kept advancing and occupying the trenches to the NE of the village and also the dead ground 300 yards in front of my position. They were evidently determined to drive us out if possible and I kept up my consolidation at top pressure. I sent back for information regarding my flanks and for SAA and bombs. I kept my H.Q. in the firing line because from there I could see the enemy's movements. As soon as SAA arrived we kept up a steady fire at the enemy as he approached us in small parties. I got news of my flanks from the Brigade and felt more confident of my position. My right flank however was still doubtful as we only had two Companies of the KRRs between us and an enemy strong point. This strong point was causing considerable trouble to the KRRs by enfilade fire along the SUNKEN ROAD. I got into communication with the KRRs and was informed that this gap was going to be made good by the 13/R.Fusiliers during the night. The enemy kept coming on in driblets all afternoon and I expected a counter-attack during the night. I sent my Lewis gun officer to select good sites for my Lewis guns, keeping two guns on each flank. My two Stokes mortars were dug in just behind the SUNKEN ROAD also protecting my flanks.*[10]

That was Drake's adventure; despite the fact that prisoners were being sparsely taken, Drake's bag of prisoners was two officers and 150 men of the 85th Infantry Regiment. Hood, on the other hand, had a very

The Sunken Lane today. This provided protection for the Drake Battalion, and a good defensive position against German counter attacks. This area later became the site of a strong point known as Towy Post. In the German March 1918 attack the post was mined and blown up.

TOWY POST   GAVRELLE   CEMETERY   MAYOR'S GAR

SUNKEN LANE
RUE DE PLOUVAIN

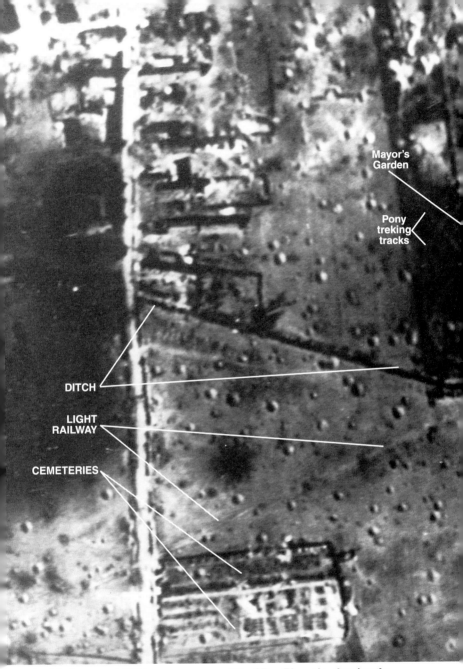

Mayor's
Garden

Pony
treking
tracks

DITCH

LIGHT
RAILWAY

CEMETERIES

Aerial photograph 'C' (see map on page 39), of Rue Plouvain showing the
two cemeteries and the ditch. Top right, darken area shows the Mayor's
Garden. The intersecting circles are pony treking tracks. Photograph
taken just before the RND attacked. (See also map 12 overleaf) (IWM)

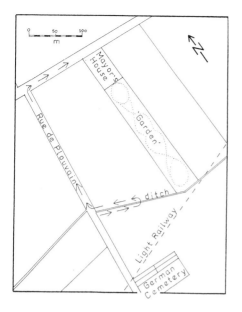

Map 12: Plan showing Asquith's route to the Mayor's House. Lieutenant Asbury was killed in the ditch, and Lieutenants Morrison and Tamplin, where killed by the same shell where the ditch joins Rue de Plouvain. Tamplin whose original grave site was just west of the cemeteries, is now in Point-du-Jour cemetery. Both Lieutenants Asbury and Morrison have no known grave.

different fight. Whereas Drake had open country to fight over, with the enemy at a fair distance, Hood's fight was in the village, at short distance, house to house. They continued the advance when the barrage lifted, when it was noted that it was hard to follow the barrage as it was at the limit of the guns and was irregular. It was also difficult

Gavrelle Church, with electric post and three poplars in foreground. Photograph taken on the yellow line, looking east.

to follow the line of the barrage as it was crashing into roofs etc instead of ground. The Hoods came out of the eastern edge of the village and found open country again. Just outside the village was the Mayor's house, on the side of the Arras-Fresnes road, which had a walled garden. 150 yards east of the Mayor's house was a trench, which was quite strongly held with supporting machine-guns and snipers. This trench was blocking the way forward, but was difficult to approach. The Mayor's house was in enemy hands, the walled garden blocked an open rush at the trench. There was a ditch which ran out from the

A prewar photograph postcard of the main road through Gavrelle.

The RND Anchor Memorial at Gavrelle.

British lines to the enemy lines and south of the offending trench. Asquith, typically in the front line, decided to take a small party down this ditch and outflank the trench:

Some of us pushed up a ditch in hopes of outflanking this enemy trench. This ditch is very shallow and at one point it is necessary to jump out over a metre gauge railway, under strong sniping at close range. The helmets of 20 to 30 Germans could be seen in this trench. Four of us went up the ditch. Lieutenant Charles Asbury and one of the two men were shot dead. It became evident that the heads of enemy occupants of this trench must be kept down if the trench were to be attacked by a flanking rush.[11]

Asbury was a tall man, over six feet high, so probably was more conspicuous in this trench[12]. Asquith looked to the Mayor's house as the next possibility for an attack on this trench. The Mayor's house was 150 yards down the Fresnes road from the cross roads where the Fresnes road crosses the Oppy road. Asquith led a party of men and burst into the house and took ten prisoners who, incredibly in the middle of a battle, were found to be asleep in the two cellars in the house. Asquith put snipers in the top story, and snipers and a Lewis gun in the rest of the house. The house offered a good view over the offending German trench and it was possible to keep the trench's garrison subdued. Asquith then rejoined the rest of the unit, leaving a little garrison behind with orders to harass the Germans. On returning to his unit Asquith had discovered that he had lost two of his senior company commanders, Lieutenants Morrison and Tamplin, who were killed by the same shell in the Rue de Plouvain.[13] A raid was mounted from the Mayor's house with a Lewis gun team on the German trench, but all bar one of the men were killed. The one survivor, Leading Seaman Charlton, continued harassing the Germans for five hours and only stopped when he ran out of ammunition; he was awarded the DCM for this. Asquith decided that an advance now onto the third objective was out of the question. The Germans held the trench in front of the Mayor's house, they had machine guns in the dead ground in front of Drake, they also held the high ground and windmill to the north east of the village, from which they were machine gunning anything that moved. Asquith found a mixed party of about 200 Nelsons and Hoods in the Oppy road on the left of Drake. Joe Murray was wounded trying to get to this point:

The next thing was to get on to the road. The mayor's house was somewhere up this road, and there was a church there. So we made for the mayor's house, at which time there were four of us or maybe five; some to the front and some to the left, but no sign of any organised advance. Just before I got to the mayor's house I was fooling around trying to get over an old door of a house. As I stood on the damned thing I slipped forward. As I went forward I saw a rifle from a cellar, but I could only see the barrel. I saw it move. Instinctively I turned quickly to the left and fired. I had a revolver. I didn't need to see the smoke from his rifle to know that I had been hit. My hand was in my pocket and the bullet went through my wrist. I couldn't get my hand out of my pocket - paralysed! I couldn't get it out.[14]

Joe Murray was helped out of Gavrelle by a German prisoner, and had to walk back to Arras along the N50 to get to the aid post; that was his service with the RND finished. Asquith sent fifty of his men back to the old German front line and got the remaining men to dig in just in front of the Oppy road, between the cemetery and the ditch. The Germans started some disorganised counter attacks, which were beaten off. It was now late morning and the day had turned into a hot one; Asquith remarked that his men were now lethargic and it was difficult to get them motivated, in stark contrast to Sterndale-Bennett's enthusiastic Drakes. The units had been in the line four days prior to the attack and were exhausted.

Drake and Hood were now dug in, the Mayor's house was still held by Hood, its small garrison in the cellar, as our own artillery had been shelling it, causing the withdrawal of many of the garrison. The main worry was the northern border of the village, which was being held by a weak force of the Bedfords. Two companies of the Nelson were sent to assist them. The situation remained the same until dusk when the Hood were relieved by Howe and returned to Point du Jour minus 200 of their comrades. 1/HAC relieved the severely weakened Royal

A Stokes Mortar and the associated equipment that had to be taken with it.

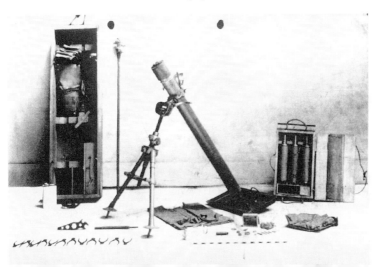

Fusiliers, and Nelson extended their line to take over from 4/Bedfords. Total casualties of the day were about 1500, amongst them in Hawke Battalion was Lieutenant A.P. Herbert RNVR, the last original from Gallipoli. He was already a famous wit and poet, after the war he would be a famous novelist and the last Independent MP to sit in the House of Commons elected as such until Martin Bell in 1997. Wounded at the same time as Herbert was the Commanding officer of Hawke, Colonel Whiteman. It transpired that Colonel Whiteman and Lieutenant Herbert and the rest of the Headquarters were moving forward. They were spotted by the Germans and this party was shelled. Both Whiteman and Herbert were wounded and were sent back for treatment. Colonel Whiteman tragically was wounded a second time and died from his wounds. 111 Brigade of 37th Division on the southern flank of the RND had a relatively successful conclusion to the day. 13/KRRC had established themselves on the right flank of Drake, continuing the occupation of the sunken road southwards, but they were out on a limb on their own. The rest of the Brigade were swung back as they had failed to take the Greenland Hill and a gap had opened between the KRRC and the rest of their division, which was rapidly filled by the 13/Rifle Brigade.

The following day would see the start of the counter attacks. Gavrelle was important and the Germans would want it back. The whole line was subjected to a very heavy bombardment, described as the heaviest the Division had ever been subjected to. The Germans then performed a mass attack along the whole front, with their artillery putting a box type barrage down to cut off the defenders. The Royal

A Lewis gun ammunition pannier found by one of the villagers while digging his garden in the 1970s.

The Lewis gun gave infantry platoons a much enhanced firepower which was used for attack and defence at Gavrelle.

Artillery, though, managed to shell the attackers, causing many casualties. The bravery of the defenders and the personal leadership of Commander Sterndale-Bennett ensured that the RND kept their prize. Sterndale-Bennett recorded these events:

> During the afternoon of 24th the enemy again appeared on the ridge to the N.E. of the village about 1000 yards away. I estimated his strength at about four battalions and, as he was shelling the village with heavies for about six hours and was putting up an intensive barrage, he evidently meant to attack the N.E. corner of the village, the most vulnerable place. The corner (MAYOR'S HOUSE) was held by a platoon of Nelsons and 1 Lewis Gun. I saw the house hit by one or two 5.9's and I saw the garrison retire. When the enemy barrage lifted I sent down to the Howe Company Commander, who was holding a line along the western edge of the cemetery, to occupy the Mayor's house at once, and sweep the ridge with a Lewis Gun in order to keep down enemy M.G's that were enfilading our trench. I sent back a message and my liaison officer to get the artillery on to the enemy on the Ridge. Just as the last wave was appearing over the ridge the artillery crashed amongst them in great style. it was a glorious sight. The enemy however were fine troops, much finer than those of the previous day, and they kept coming on by occupying shell holes and small trenches. Our Lewis Guns and rifles on the left flank played havoc with these parties and were keeping up a steady well-controlled fire, which mowed down the enemy. I thought that probably the enemy troops that were just in front were waiting for those on my left flank to get up into line before advancing. Just as the enemy was getting up into line I sent up my S.O.S. and the barrage came down on those in front of my position. They held on and suffered badly from this barrage. Any that moved were mowed down by my men.[15]

Up to the north of Gavrelle Lt Haine of 1/HAC was also involved in the German counter attacks:

> We wondered what on earth was happening because we saw all these troops and that sort of thing coming up in column of fours. They were outside the range of our artillery – our normal artillery at any rate. So we got a bit perturbed about this and got on the wire - I suppose the CO did or something. They said 'Well, it looks like a German attack. But don't worry, it's all taped'. And it was taped. I've never seen such a fiasco in all my life. They came on in mass on a glorious April afternoon, the 24th, and

they came down line after line of them and our gunners they just let into them and we had practically nothing to do. As a matter of fact it was a Prussian Guards Division who did this attack and they came on very gallantly but of course it was absolutely hopeless.[16]

Gavrelle was now in the hands of the RND; Commander Sterndale-Bennett:

I feel that I am not exaggerating when I estimate the enemy's casualties at two thousand. We were firing at them continually all the time we were up there, the fire was well controlled and splendid effects were seen - The artillery was magnificent, the enemy was thoroughly butchered and we enjoyed every moment of it all.[17]

The Official History of the Great War gives an excellent assessment of the achievement of the RND, a formation which is almost anonymous in popular history:

Full justice has not been done to the achievement of the 63rd Division, because the details of the street fighting in which it showed skill and determination are too intricate for description. The division had taken 479 prisoners and in defeating the counter-attacks had obviously inflicted heavy loss upon the enemy.[18]

On 26 April, the battalions of 188 Brigade, minus the Howe Battalion, took over the line, with the addition of 1/HAC. Their task was to protect the gains from the numerous small counter attacks, and on the 28th to complete the job that the RND were tasked to do on 23 April.

1. Murray, J. Taped Interview, reel 41, Dept of Sound Archives, Imperial War Museum
2. Bernard Freyberg was awarded the Victoria Cross for bravery at Beaucourt, 13 November 1916
3. Raymond Asquith was wounded with 3/Grenadier Guards and died of these wounds, 15 September 1916.
4. Murray, J. *op cit*
5. Sterndale-Bennett, W. Account of Gavrelle fighting in his Army book 152
6. Hood Battalion War Diary, PRO ADM137/3064
7. Murray, J.
8. Hood Battalion War Diary,
9. Lieutenant Colonel Collings-Wells was awarded the Victoria Cross posthumously in March 1918
10. Sterndale-Bennett, W.
11. Hood Battalion War Diary,
12. Lieutenant C.P .Asbury RNVR has no known grave and his name is on the Arras Memorial to the Missing
13. Lieutenant J.W.Morrison RNVR has no known grave and his name is on the Arras Memorial to the Missing. Lieutenant G.H.Tamplin RNVR was buried within Gavrelle and after the war reburied at Point du Jour British Cemetery.
14. Murray, J.
15. Sterndale-Bennett, W.
16. Haine, R.L. Taped interview, Dept of Sound Archives Imperial War Museum
17. Sterndale-Bennett, W.
18. Falls, C., *Official History of the Great War Military Operations France and Belgium 1917* Volume 1, p 400

Chapter Three

CONSOLIDATION

In the days after 23 April the German artillery was very active, constantly trying to blast the RND out of their gains. On 28 April a second British attack around Gavrelle was planned. The purpose of this attack was to act in support to the Canadian Corps and 2nd Division attacking to the north at Arleux and Oppy Wood respectively. Its objectives were to take the windmill and the high ground to the north east of Gavrelle, which were barring any advance out of, and threatening the British hold on, Gavrelle. Lastly it was to support 37th Division, who were to attack Greenland Hill to the south. The operation was in three distinct parts and would be carried out by 188 Brigade, which had been spared on 23 April; 1/HAC was attached from 190 Brigade for support.

1/Royal Marines Light Infantry was required to form a defensive flank for the 2nd Division on its left, thus protecting that Division's right flank. This would be done by an advance in three stages, capturing three German lines and penetrating to a depth of 1000 yards. 1/RM would start its attack from just north of Gavrelle with its left hand flank in contact with units of the 2nd Division, whilst its right hand company would be astride the railway line and remain so until the German support line was reached. The first objective was some unfinished trenches behind the German front line. The next step would be to send fighting patrols out whilst the 2nd Division took its second objective; when that was done 1/RM would advance to come along side it. The third and final objective was in line with the 2nd Division's third objective. 1/RM was to advance to this spot, stop and consolidate, linking with the 2nd Division units to the north and 2/RM to the south. This attack was independent of the attack by other units of 188 Brigade. The 2nd Division and the Canadians were trying to breach the Arleux Loop defensive system. Gavrelle was part of this defensive system but the RND's role was purely a supportive one. The Arleux Loop was the last formed defensive system in front of the partially completed Siegfied Line, breaching it therefore would jeopardise the Germans defensive plan. 1/RM's sector was from just to the south of Oppy Wood to the northern edge of Gavrelle itself. This not only included the front occupied by the whole of 190 Brigade on the 23rd, but was even longer as 1/RM had taken over some of the 2nd Division's front also.

See map 14 page 57

The Mayor's Garden in the 1990s. In 1917, as today, it is an ornamental garden, with pony treking tracks. There was a small cluster of graves in the garden after the Great War consisting of Able Seamen Bromley and Relf of the Nelson Battalion, four unknown Ansons, and three unknown British soldiers. All nine are now in Orchard Dump Cemetery.

The second part of the assault was to be carried out by 2/RM. The plan was to advance out of Gavrelle and advance down the axis of the Fresnes road to a depth of 700 yards. 2/RM would start from within Gavrelle village and had two separate objectives. The first objective was the windmill on the high ground to the north east, a platoon was assigned to this task. The other objective was a group of unfinished trenches to the south of the Gavrelle-Izel road. This would bring them alongside the 1/RM third objective. Some of these unfinished trenches extended north of this road, 2/RM were instructed to leave these until 1/RM's artillery barrage had passed that point, then patrol up and take and consolidate these trenches. 2/RM on their final objective were to dig in and consolidate, linking with 1/RM to the north and Anson to the south. This would support the 37th Division, to the south of the RND.

The last part of the attack would be performed by C Company of the Anson Battalion. This unit would follow after 2/RM and peel off to the south to form a flank guard, as there was still an enemy presence just outside Gavrelle in this area. Anson's task was to protect the southern flank and to form a link from the cemetery, south of Gavrelle, to the final objective of 2/RM.

Before the attack Folly, Falcon and Flabby trenches were to be evacuated to allow the artillery to cut the wire. As soon as the main attack commenced 1/HAC were to occupy these trenches. Whilst those trenches were unoccupied, mortar and rifle grenade fire was to be

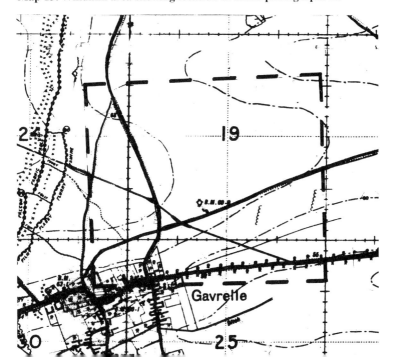

'A' - WINDMILL TRENCH   'C' - RAILWAY TRENCH   'D' - WINDMILL MAZE
'B' - WINDMILL SUPPORT   'E' - GAVRELLE TRENCH

! STRONG POINT REPORTED BY PATROLS.

M.G's FROM HERE ENFILADED TROOPS ADVANCING S OF OPPY WOOD. ALSO REPORTED BY PATROL.

M.G. NEST.

NOTE TRACKS LEADING TO DUGOUTS.

M.G' HERE.

TRENCH MORTAR POSITION HERE NOW OBLITERATED.

POSTS CONNECTING UP TWO TRENCH LINES.

OLD TELEPHONE DUGOUT.

SIGNAL BOX.

SUPPORTING POINTS.

WINDMILL.

GAVRELLE →

HOUSES REPORTED UNOCCUPIED. NOW BUT HELD DURING LAST ATTACK.

4. M.G' ROUND HERE.

TRENCH REQUIRES CAREFUL MOPPING UP. THERE IS A TUNNEL DUGOUT WHERE GERMANS REMAINED CONCEALED IN PREVIOUS ATTACK.

Annotated aerial photograph of the windmill area north of Gavrelle. The photograph was taken on 2 May 1917. These photographs provided valuable information on recently captured areas, where trenches and strongpoints were rapidly being established, making previous trench maps of the area outdated.

Map 13. Windmill area showing location of aerial photograph. PRO

conducted on Foggy trench to keep the Germans from coming south of that point. Machine guns were placed on Hill 80 behind 1/RM's position to fire overhead, machine guns were in 1/RM's line also as support. Machine guns were placed in the north east of Gavrelle to enfilade the Germans, others were put in the south east of the cemetery in Anson's sector. A section of machine guns were also to go over the top with each of the Royal Marine battalions. Stokes and medium trench mortars were also to be used. Medium mortars were placed in the north east of Gavrelle to pound the area to the north of 2/RM's starting line until 1/RM's artillery barrage reached that point. Two stokes mortars were to advance with each of the two assaulting units to give local fire support, a section was also retained with 1/HAC as a reserve. A section of Royal Engineers were attached to the assaulting units. Lastly the artillery support assigned to the attack was considerable, consisting of six field artillery brigades plus Corps and heavy artillery brigades. The RFC were to overfly the area to monitor progress and the attacking waves had a series of flares to fire to signal progress.

Even during the evening before the battle the Germans were still active, as Able Seaman Downe of Anson noted:

The sun faded behind the woods around Fresnes - les - Montauban and a strange feeling of restlessness came over me as I gazed over the parapet at its glorious crimson setting, only to be swept back into the crucible of shattered dreams as the full blast of the enemy's barrage came upon us again. It was a repetition of the morning's agony, and later we heard that the Marines had again smashed the German attempt to advance. Another long night, during which we were troubled by the non-arrival of our rations.[1]

The morning of the 28th came and the various attacks started, each of them, unusually, very much complete in themselves.

1/RM's Attack

In the early hours of the 28th at 4.25am the attack started and little more was ever heard from 1/RM. On 1/RM's front it was found that the wire was uncut and strong, not a good omen. Their start line was also not taped out, so they prolonged the line of the 13/Essex of the 2nd Division on their left. During the night they were shelled causing casualties, but still worse making communications and ration collecting nearly impossible. How the day's events unfolded is covered baldly by a two-line entry in the Battalion War Diary:

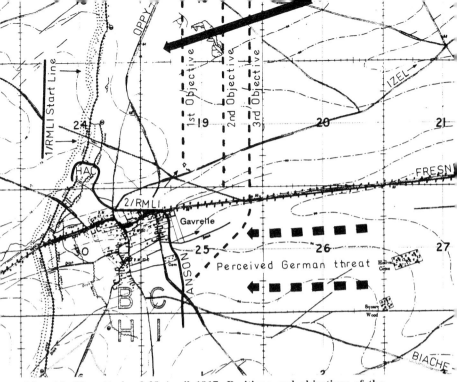

Map 14: The attack of 28 April 1917. Positions and objectives of the RMLI. PRO

Bttn attacked on sector left of Gavrelle-Oppy line at 4.25am.
Gained objective but were driven out by counter attacks.[2]

The attack started on time but, as the wire in front of the German lines was found to be uncut on the south (Gavrelle side) of the sector, many men settled in shell holes in front of the German line and conducted the firefight from there. The wire on the north side of the sector was better cut so the axis of the attack took the path of least resistance and headed left (northwards). This meant that the German strongpoint at the corner of Fabric and Folly Trenches, instead of being tackled head on, was now to the south of the attack and was in a position to enfilade the Royal Marines: this was a repetition of what happened to 190 Brigade units on 23 April. Many marines were therefore shot down quickly and the attack began to falter badly. At 6.30 am 1/ HAC were ordered to attack northwards along the trenches towards this strongpoint and engage it with Stokes mortars. To remove this strongpoint would enable a link to be established with 1/RM. Around this time units of the 2nd Division had taken the first two objectives but had not seen 1/RM. Consequently their right flank was open so they had formed a defensive flank facing south. Just after 7am, 1/HAC

57

had cleared Flurry and Flabby trench. Still nothing was known about 1/RM from either side of the attack. 1/ HAC were aware that there was serious fighting going on to the north, and the fact that the Germans still held their first line. The 2nd Division was trying to bomb down it to reach them. As Lieutenant Haine, soon to be awarded the Victoria Cross, recalls:

> At any rate we went along to this blockade where the railway was and the attack started and nothing happened. We could see these fellows, fifty yards on our left the nearest of them were. They were getting hung up on the wire and it was absolutely hopeless. They were a battalion of Marines, but they, poor chaps, could not get through the wire. And then Ossy, our colonel, said 'Well, you've got to do something about it! So I was told to attack laterally along this trench. Well, I tried once or twice.[3]

1/ HAC were also having no joy attacking the strongpoint, the ground around it was flat and swept by machine-guns and snipers, whilst the German stick grenades were outranging the mills bombs. Rifle grenades were then sent for. At 7:15am the first news of 1/RM was received at headquarters and that was that a wounded marine of the 4th wave said that the wire was very strong but that the others had got through and gone on. A plane overflying the area reported seeing a group of around twenty Marines in the first objective. They fired flares to alert the plane, which was the signal agreed, which does show that

RMLI during the Great War, (unit and battalion not known).

elements of 1/RM got through the wire. The only source of information available was from the wounded, which was usually out of date. However, the information was that the first two waves of 1/RM got to their objectives, but were then hit hard by a massive counter attack from the direction of Oppy Wood (ie from the north). The right hand battalion of the 2nd Division was overpowered and so were the marines, despite severe hand to hand fighting. The Germans had a large numerical advantage and the attackers were ejected or killed and were now back in their starting lines. It was now coming up to 9am and 1/HAC finally took the strongpoint:

Well, my fellows, I mean, I'm talking about me but it was the company; And eventually we fanned out a bit as far as the wire round the left and I was having wonderful support from Pat O'Brien on my right who was in the German support line. Eventually we got into this strong point and we found quite a lot of German dead there and also a certain number of German living- I think it was about fifty - Germans, we got them back.[4]

It was too late though; the damage had been done, 1/HAC proceeded to work northwards in order to get in touch with friendly troops. It was not in contact with 1/RM but individual marines joined them. The 2nd Division was not sure of where 1/RM were. The truth was 1/RM was now effectively wiped out, with remnants holding its jumping off trench, with isolated pockets of men trapped behind the German counter attack. An overflying aircraft saw a flare from 1/RM's second objective at 9:40am The Germans were now hitting back in force, the attack had failed and the few surviving attackers were now defenders. Germans were now counter attacking in the region of the jumping off trenches, and continuing southwards down their old front line. By 10:20am the troublesome strongpoint was back in German hands.

We'd got very few troops. Then the Boche started a really hectic counter attack. He was coming up from his own support lines and getting round us, They were far too strong for us. They were Prussian Guards and they infiltrated up the side trenches and I was terrified that we were going to be completely surrounded. So we decided that discretion was the better part of valour and we scrambled back - you can't call it anything else - to where we started from, the block in the trench where we'd started from that morning.[5]

Twenty minutes later Germans were reported west of the British old front line, it looked like the RND were going to end up losing ground. The situation was now serious, the northern attack was now a defensive battle for survival. At 12:30pm, 1/HAC had formed a strong defence around Folly trench, the Howe battalion was ordered up to the hill behind 1/RMs jumping off trench, 14/Worcester, the RND's Pioneer Battalion, were put on short notice to move and 18/DLI of the 31st Division were also earmarked to come up in support. Little is reported of what happened next except that the Germans pushed probing patrols steadily westwards but seemed reluctant to test a weak line. The RFC reported various signal flares in the 1/RM sector of attack, but these gradually tailed off as one little garrison after another was overcome. By nightfall, 1/HAC held the majority of the old 1/RM front line with the Howe close by, 18/DLI were on Hill 80 behind the old front line. Things were back to where they started in the morning, only that 1/RM had virtually ceased to exist.

2/RM's Attack

The southern attack by 2/RM commenced on time at 4:25am; Anson were to follow later and peel off southwards to form defensive strongpoints. The wire was found to be cut only in one place and A, C and D companies of 2/RM poured through. At 7am it was reported from a wounded man that the Windmill and first trench objectives had been taken and the final objective was under attack. The Windmill was captured by 5 Platoon of B Company under Lieutenant Newling. There was heavy machine gun fire and sniping from both flanks and therefore no information could be got back. At 7:25am it was reported that 2/RM had taken all of its objectives but had sustained many casualties getting thus far. At around 5am C company of Anson moved out to perform their task but got into difficulty virtually immediately as, 400 yards in front of the front line near to the Gavrelle-Fresnes road, there was a strongpoint which was resisting with machine gun and rifle fire. At 8:30am thirty prisoners were sent down from the Windmill, whilst at the same time final confirmation was received that all

A German postcard showing the Windmill at Gavrelle.

Windmühle bei Gavrelle.

60

objectives were taken. Anyone, including stretcher bearers, that moved in the open were machine gunned or sniped at, whilst rather ominously they were being subjected to machine gun fire from both flanks and there was no sign of 1/RM to their north. At 10:10am the Windmill was subjected to a counter attack by about 150 of the enemy, but it was not seriously pressed home and was beaten off with the help of the artillery. At around this time the rest of 2/RM were starting to be counter attacked. Things were starting to go awry, B company of 2/RM could not fight their way through the original gap and were forced to dig in, in the old German front line. The Germans were pressing hard on both flanks of 2/RM which was deep into a salient that they had created. It seemed that A, C and D companies of 2/RM were in a bag, which was being drawn shut. By 11:30am these three companies were in effect cut off, B company held the old German front line, the jumping off trench was held by two privates and the quartermaster sergeant, whilst the Windmill still held solid and another hundred prisoners were sent in from there. The Germans massed several times to counter attack the windmill, but on each occasion the Royal Artillery broke up these formations. Things

Private McMurdo 2/RMLI – captured at Gavrelle.

reached a stalemate as things quietened down a bit as both sides took stock of the situation. The three companies of 2/RM were forced to surrender, as there was no hope of relief. This fact is mentioned in the Official History of the War. Its source is German, the account is exaggerated but gives the gist of what happened:

> A British battalion with machine guns was seen advancing along the Gavrelle-Fresnes road, north of the regimental sector. The machine gun company of the right hand battalion took this column and its line of retreat under such effective fire that it surrendered as a body to the division to our right.[6]

At 2:10pm the Germans massed again to the east of Gavrelle and yet again the artillery saved the day. At 2:30pm the Commanding Officer of 2/RM conceded that his men were now holding only the old German front line, the Windmill, which had been reinforced, and some men cut off in the final objective. Major Eagles, the commander of B Company, visited the Windmill several times to

An artists impression of fighting at Gavrelle Windmill.

assess the situation[7]. The commanding officer of 2/RM decided to link
the old German front line to the Windmill, by digging up to the latter;
so he asked for a company of 4/Bedfords. This request was granted, but
there would be some time before they got there. At around this time the
Germans went for another attack at the Windmill, which once more
was repulsed with large losses. The enemy massed to attack three more
times to the east of Gavrelle and each time the artillery broke it up. The
Germans now sat on the situation for a while. Their losses in
concentrating to attack had obviously been great.

A plane over Gavrelle at 7pm saw a flare in a pre-arranged signal
from the 2/RM final objective; it meant that a small pocket of
resistance was still there but was now completely cut off with no hope
of rescue. The Germans launched one final attack on 2/RM and Anson
at 8:30pm and this was beaten off, again with the help of artillery. That
evening 14/Worcesters came up and took over the line of Anson and
2/RM, perfectly illustrating that the pioneers were also fighting troops.
That was the end of the attack on the 2/RM front. There were still 40
Royal Marines of 2/RM holding the Windmill and outposts around it;
in all they had repulsed thirteen counter attacks. The casualties of
2/RM had been even more severe than those of 1/RM at the end of the
day.

Anson Battalion's ordeal

Able Seaman Downe's description provides the basis for the account of the actions of Anson on this day.[8] Anson followed out behind 2/RM but soon encountered problems with machine-guns from the direction of the Douai road:

Able Seaman Downe.

> We edged along the trench, and in the fire-bay by the garden of the mayor's house Bradley directed us into the ditch. These ditches were actually drains for the surface water from the village, and this particular one was a continuation of that along which Walton and I had crept to gain the front line. It ran past Pollard's bombing post, across No Man's Land, hugging the line of the mayor's garden, and petered away in the fields towards Fresnes, and was about three feet deep. An officer, Carter, led the party on hands and knees and there were a dozen men from the platoon in front of me, when we became held up in a block caused by a light gauge railway crossing the ditch at an angle, causing the filling in of twenty feet or so.[9]

This ditch was the same ditch that Asquith travelled down on his attempt to enfilade an enemy trench on the 23rd.

> The first four men jumped into the open and dashed across, but three were immediately hit, a machine-gun appearing to open at them from the mayor's garden right in advance of the German line. The company behind us were crowding into the ditch, so Carter ordered a headlong dash by as many of the party as possible. With my heart beating at a tremendous pace I held my breath and made a frantic dash. Wonderful luck-the machine-gun fired short, the bullets tearing up the dust round my feet, while a revolver bullet spat by my ear. I covered the distance in about three leaps, but fell on top of Wilmer, who had been hit, and was lying on the other side. In a few minutes ten men and Carter were over the railway, and as no more appeared to be making a move the officer continued the advance. Thirty yards further he halted and ordered the party out into the open into the nearest shell hole.[10]

At 7:30 am Anson were in serious trouble, the enemy were seen to advance and were opening a heavy fire and Anson were taking heavy casualties, so much so that Anson's commanding officer ordered up another company and put another on standby. They also had not found

Private A Higgins 1/RMLI, from Ashford, Kent. Killed in action 28 April 1917.

the flank of 2/RM where they believed it would be. This company of Anson was out on a limb now and were being subjected to tremendous shelling.

We immediately reposed in the earth once again, for the enemy started shelling the ditch. A terrific crash came from a few yards to our rear, and as I looked over my shoulder I saw two men without heads. Another shell fell nearer, and Tommy Galbraith and I thudded together and whirled over on our backs. Shells fell with uncertainty around the ditch, but were concentrated in full blast on the front line trench. No further members of the company had reinforced us, and those not risking the railway crossing retired to the trench where this inferno was raging. Bradley shouted above the din to Carter and asked him whether we should follow. Carter replied that they were ensconced in a shell hole a few yards away, but gave no definite instructions as to our further movements.[11]

The situation was that the defensive series of outposts that was meant to secure 2/RM's flank were not in place and 2/RM were exposed. Downe actually witnessed the start of the surrender of a few Marines:

The firing ceased as suddenly as it had begun, and peeping up I found that the Germans had disappeared, but the gunfire was still feeling around the rather vaguely outlined series of pits forming the German support line. Khaki figures crossed the ditch behind the enemy line – Marines with their hands up, and it looked as if the flank of the attack was giving way.[12]

The situation remained unchanged for an hour or so but at 10am Anson still had not secured the 2/RM flank and had suffered badly in the attempt, so their commanding officer decided to withdraw them. This was easier said than done, the company as a whole certainly could not do it, it was more a matter of every man for himself, using the ditches and drains that were around Gavrelle:

I lay still, wondering how on earth I was going to get clear. The German was about twenty yards away. I listened for movement amid the desultory gunfire and heard none, nor rifle fire from that direction. I felt that it was no good lying there, and peeped cautiously up. Shovelfuls of earth were being thrown up, and I saw the German's " pork pie" cap as he bent and rose at his task. He was building a barricade. Now was the time to act- it was no good leaving things until a sentry was posted. I considered the distance an eighty yards scramble back to Carter

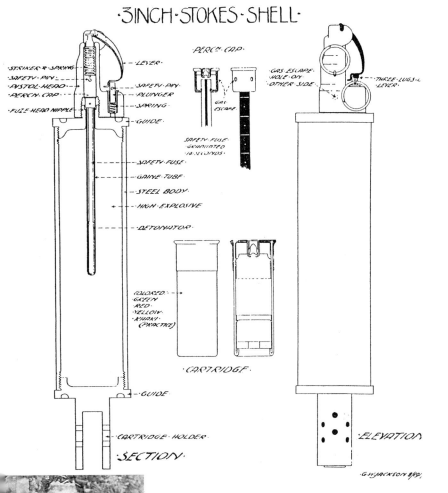

·3 INCH·STOKES·SHELL·

·PERCⁿ·CAP·

- STRIKER SPRING
- SAFETY PIN
- PISTOL HEAD
- PERCⁿ CAP
- FUZE HEAD NIPPLE
- LEVER
- SAFETY PIN
- PLUNGER
- SPRING
- GUIDE
- SAFETY FUSE
- GAINE TUBE
- STEEL BODY
- HIGH EXPLOSIVE
- DETONATOR
- GUIDE
- CARTRIDGE HOLDER

·SECTION·

GAS ESCAPE

SAFETY FUSE GRADUATED 18 SECONDS

COLORED
GREEN
RED
YELLOW
KHAKI
(PRACTICE)

·CARTRIDGE·

GAS ESCAPE HOLE ON OTHER SIDE

THREE LUGS LEVER

·ELEVATION·

G.W.JACKSON 9/81

Three inch stokes mortar shell. The Stokes mortar shell was fused in roughly a similar way to a Mills bomb. Put simply, it operated as follows:

1. A shotgun like cartridge was inserted into the base of the shell.

2. The two pins were removed from the shell and the shell was dropped into the tube of the mortar.

3. The shell slid down the tube where a pin in the base of the tube struck the shotgun cartridge propelling the shell.

4. The force of the shell being propelled released the lever in the fuse, whilst in the mortar tube. The lever stayed with the shell. Once out of the tube the lever flew off the shell and the fuse started, in a similar way to that of a Mill's bomb

5. The shell goes toward the target where it explodes on a timed rather than impact basis.

6. A skilled team could have four shells in the air at once!

PRO

and the rest of the party, I felt for my rifle, sprang up and made a dash. I reached Singleton's body and took a flying leap over to where I hoped the shell hole was, and fortunately rolled into it. The party showed no signs of alarm at my sudden arrival, the events of the day evidently had erased in them all elements of surprise. I sat on the sloping edge of the hole, wiped my sweating brow with my sleeve and looked at them, What a dismal crowd! Only Galbraith was interested to inquire as to how I had been spending the previous hour. Having regained my breath, I made an enquiry of Carter as to what we were going to do next. He promptly informed me that we were going to stop where we were and crawl back to the line at dusk. I then proceeded to inform him in detail of our adventures in the ditch and he looked really alarmed. Did the Germans know that we were here? If so, they would be sure to send a strong party forward at dusk. Carter, who wishing to gather together the remnants of the company, the majority of which were expected to be in the front line, decided on a general withdrawal to that line, especially in view of the fact that somebody had found that a large-bore stoneware drain ran under the railway, through which there was a possibility of us crawling. I did not feel from the start at all enthusiastic at negotiating nearly twenty-five feet of piping, but, like everybody else, was quite prepared to ignore natural dislikings for safety. Guns of various calibres were still barking, although we had no immediate feeling of fear at the presence of the German machine-gun crew on the fringe of the mayor's garden. The bodies lying on the railway turned our thoughts to the uneasy hours that had passed. Various people disappeared into the pipe, and as I was on the tail end of the party I sat and munched some biscuits. I stuffed the remaining biscuits in my haversack, stripped my webbing equipment and tied it round one of my ankles. Unfixing my bayonet, I wedged it into its scabbard and followed Andrews, after giving him a few minutes start. I decided to push my rifle in front of me. One man remained, Carter. I asked him if he would prefer to precede me, but he motioned me to hurry through. My shoulders were not over-wide, but I just got in; my arms, bent at the elbows, were squeezed tightly, so that it was impossible to push them over my head. I could only make progress with the movements of my legs, and progress was slow. Andrews was still in the pipe and I could not see daylight at that end, while Carter had followed me quickly, for I could feel his

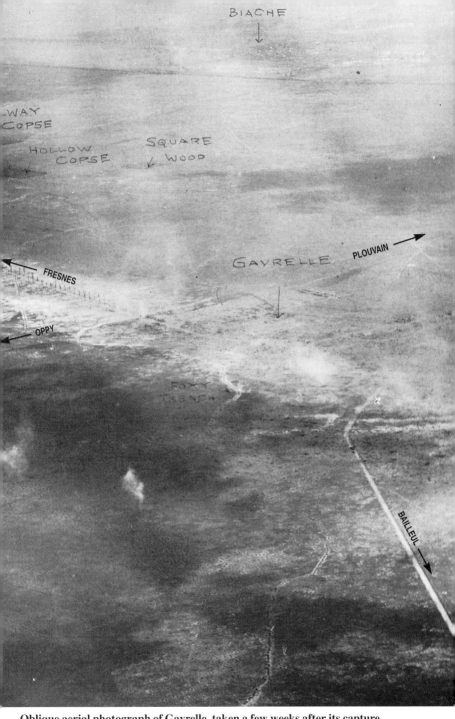

BIACHE

-WAY
COPSE

HOLLOW
COPSE

SQUARE
WOOD

FRESNES

GAVRELLE

PLOUVAIN

OPPY

FOXY
TRENCH

BAILLEUL

Oblique aerial photograph of Gavrelle, taken a few weeks after its capture by the RND. The village is in ruins, and the Gavrelle-Fresnes road heavily shelled. This photograph is looking south-east, and under the annotation of 'Gavrelle' can be seen the Mayor's Garden, the ditch and walled cemetery. (RM Museum)

head against my feet. Exertion left me breathless, and with the air almost blocked at both ends and sweat pouring into my eyes, which I could not wipe, my head began to whirl. I was suddenly alarmed-my foot held tightly to something. I tugged it was the leg with the equipment attached. Something was caught-my bayonet scabbard, seemingly, in a broken joint of the pipe. Daylight appeared at the far end. Andrews was out. I shouted, but what was the use? My leg was held in a vice. I jerked and pulled, and a pain shot through my wrenched hip. I went limp and lay helplessly looking at the circular opening showing daylight. Terror-stricken, I pulled the equipment till it twisted like a knot round my ankle, while against my feet Carter's head nosed. Thoughts raced through my mind- horrible imaginings. I felt too weak to pull -And what was the use? Carter was tight against my feet I could not ease myself backward to loosen the grip. Carter must have been in a worse plight. A huge fellow, how he got into the pipe I never knew, and he had no air. His head, down at my feet, in a frenzy urged me on. Minutes passed. I gained renewed energy, and then fell exhausted.

Strength seemed to come in bursts, and while my brain remained clear I fought to retain my energy so did the officer behind. His head beat against the obstacle, which barred his progress, loosened the bayonet, pushing my legs against the sides of the pipe. I was free, and with seeming ease, worked my way forward and out again into the ditch, where I lay gasping amongst several wounded.[13]

This account is fairly typical of the individual battles for survival. One party was cut off and came back after dark driving 250 prisoners between themselves and the Germans, using the prisoners as a human shield. That was the end of the advance for Anson's C company. Anson was subjected to counter attacks for the rest of the day until relieved by 14/Worcester that evening.

On the flank of Anson, 111 Brigade had some success. The front line attacking units were 13/Royal Fusiliers and 13/Rifle Brigade. The objective was to take the Gavrelle-Plouvain road, and 63 Brigade on their right was to take Greenland Hill. 111 Brigade took their objectives and, more importantly, took the crossroads formed where the road from Fampoux crosses the Gavrelle-Plouvain road. Things then went wrong, units of 63 Brigade got lost and crossed behind the 13/Royal Fusiliers and went through them and off into a north easterly direction. They took many of 111 Brigade with them. This force went

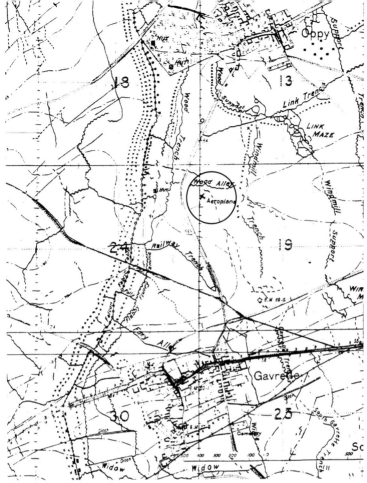

Map 15: Trench map of the area between Gavrelle and Oppy, updated with new trenches. Note the crashed aeroplane, a valuable landmark in the disorientating lunar landscape of shell holes. PRO

through Square Wood and onto Railway Copse. It was from here that the enemy made his counter attacks and it looked like these off course forces would walk into a hornets' nest. Control was restored, and many of these men were called back, but unfortunately Greenland Hill was still in German hands.

The attacks around Gavrelle had failed because of miscalculation by higher command. They honestly believed that opposition would be light, hence two battalions were ordered to attack a greater frontage than two brigades a few days before. In the case of 1/RM many bodies were found after the war just behind the German front line. 1/RM had experienced the German tactic of lightly holding the front line and counter attacking violently once an attack developed. 2/RM's main

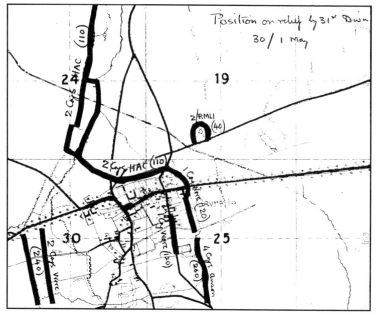

Map 16: Positions held by the units of the RND on the night of 30 April 1917. The numbers in the brackets indicate troop strength. <small>PRO</small>

attack failed because they advanced deeper into an already developed salient with both flanks exposed. The battle post mortem by Brigadier-General Prentice is revealing, firstly in the fact that higher authority believed that the Germans held the area weakly:

> *The enemy undoubtedly had reserves ready for the counter attack and were evidently much stronger than I was given to suppose by the BGGS of the 13th [sic] Corps, when discussing the operations at my headquarters, previous to the issue of orders by Division.*[14]

He goes on to push the point about the lack of opposition and the fact that he had anticipated problems and his countermeasures were vetoed:

> *I was informed at the conversation referred to above, that little or no opposition was to be expected. This I think could have been avoided, as I suggested at the time, had an attack been made from the line south of the cemetery in conjunction with the main attack.*[15]

The battalions themselves appeared to be under no illusions as to what lay in store for them, especially after witnessing first hand the events of 23 April, and the vicious counter attacks since. One entry in attack orders sums it up aptly:

> *All indications and information lead to the assumption that the enemies troops have orders to oppose strenuously our advance on the north bank of the Scarpe, which, if successful,*

70

not only brings us up to the Siegfried line before it's completed but also threatens his hold on Lens. Violent counter attacks must therefore be expected and will probably develop very shortly after we reach our final objective.[16]

Things at the end of the day were virtually the same as at the start, except that the strategically important Windmill position and the high ground it stood on had been taken and held. The rest of the front line was the same, except that the two Royal Marine battalions had been hammered, along with a company of Anson Battalion. In the following days, when all of these units were out of the line, the grim reckoning took place as to what happened to many of the men. An eye witness, Private Hubert Trotman of 2/RM, describes it:

The General and his staff were sitting at the table and the few of us that come back from Arras, he gathered us around and he knew who the dead were who had been picked up and who the wounded were that had gone back but what he was worrying about was the missing men. 'Who was last to see Sergeant so and so', and somebody would give a reply, 'I saw him' etc. Anyway lots of names of officers and men were missing and he went through them.[17]

The Cost

The losses for the Royal Marines Light Infantry were, and still are, the largest casualty list for one day's fighting in its history, which amounted to 850 all ranks with a high fatal to wounded ratio of almost one to one, whereas it would be normally one to three. Amongst the casualties were some notable people. Private Horace Bruckshaw, whose diaries have been edited by Martin Middlebrook, was killed in the Windmill area. The Commanding Officer of 1/RM, Lieutenant-Colonel Cartwright, died of his wounds, and amongst the dead was Lieutenant Edgar Lovell Filmer Platts of 1/RM. This officer has been singled out because, to the best of the authors' knowledge, he was the youngest officer to be killed with the British Army during the Great War at the age of seventeen.

Private Horace Bruckshaw and wife.

Edgar Lovell Filmer Platts was born on 18 June 1899 in Cambridge, the son of a senior clergyman. He was educated at St Faith's and Christ's Hospital. Apparently, soon after the war broke out whilst on school holidays, he was presented with a white feather by a girl, as he appeared to be of military age and appearance. In April 1915 he enlisted in the RNVR for service with the RND, he gave his year of birth as 1896, his true age however was only fifteen. His service records give his height as being 5ft 8 inches; although not a giant, he was tall and mature, apparently known as 'Tiny' amongst his friends. Within two months he was transferred to the Royal Marines Light Infantry, to serve in the cyclists' section. He must have made an impression, because in September 1915 he was offered a commission into the RMLI. Therefore he was a Second Lieutenant at the age of sixteen. His training continued and he was sent to France in April 1916 to see the trenches. On his return he was sent with a Royal Marine battalion to Ireland to cover the troubles; active service overseas, as an officer, at the age of sixteen seems incredible. On his return home in May 1916 he was immediately transferred to France and 1/RM, which had just arrived from the Balkans. Platts was only just seventeen at this point. He was promoted to lieutenant in September. Platts was accidentally slightly wounded by a grenade in early November 1916 and took part in the Battle of the Ancre on 13 November, in which he was again wounded, indeed he was one of the few officers left alive. He recuperated at home and returned to active service in February 1917, just after the RND's next major engagement at Miraumont. Platts at this point was probably one of the senior lieutenants in his battalion,

The Senior NCO's of 2/RMLI just before the capture of Gavrelle. All bar two became casulties on 28 April 1917. Back Row: Sgt Taylor, Sgt Ludbrooke name unknown, name unknown. Middle Row: Sgt Wagner, Sgt Quinn CSM Milne, RSM unknown, name unknown. Front Row: name unknown, Sgt Alvey. RM. MUSEUM

Obituary of Lieutenant Platts which appeared in The Times. Right: Lieutenant Platts. (Mrs M. Clarke)

indeed his commanding officer wrote to his mother after his death saying that he was shortly to be promoted to captain. On the day of Gavrelle it is not known in which company Platts was serving , or what exactly happened to him. All we do know is that a boy was leading a group of men much older than him into a perilous situation at an age when modern children are combating exams. On 4 August 1917 his obituary appeared in *The Times*, giving his biography and his real date of birth. Ironically it was in the same week that *The Times* carried Sassoon's protest letter against the war, it even forms a paragraph of Pat Barkers 'Regeneration', where Sassoon reads out Platts obituary and age, pointing out that Platts was too young to enlist. Strangely enough, the write up of the Gavrelle story in 'Britain's Sea Soldiers', which is the RMLI official history, lists all the officers killed or missing at the battle, but Platts name is missing, the only one. Platts body was not identified after the war and his name appears on the Arras Memorial to the Missing.

29 April, Two Victoria Crosses for the HAC

The following days 1/HAC were ordered to attack the trenches where defenders had wiped out the Royal Fusiliers on the 23rd and 1/RM the day before. The difference this time would be that the attack would be roughly two companies in size, and instead of being a frontal assault, it would be made at right angles to the axis of the trench, i.e. a grander scale of what Lieutenant Haine did on the 28th. Haine was again selected, with his much depleted company, to attack and take the strongpoint and the trenches beyond it; with him would be Lieutenant Alfred Pollard, who already gained the DCM whilst serving in the ranks, and had won the MC twice. Haine describes the day's events:

73

Lieutenant N I Lion 1/RMLI, killed in Action 28 April 1917. His body, along with 12 others, were found by a patrol and buried at Viscount Street cemetery. The graves in this cemetery were concentrated into Orchard Dump Cemetery, but Lion could not be identified, and his name is on the Arras Memorial to the Missing.

I remember about some time before dawn – I don't know when it was – a runner came up and said the CO wanted to see me. Ossy, that was our colonel, Colonel Osmond, he said "Well, Bill", he said, "you've got to do it again!" I said "Good God!" He said, "Yes". I said, "Well what about 2 Company?" – because 2 Company had been held in reserve around battalion headquarters the whole time and they were a company intact, you see. I shall never forget him, he said, "Bill, I dare not risk it". He said, "You've got to do it". So I said, "Very good, sir", or words to that effect, and went back. Well, at dawn we managed to scrape a couple of mortars from somewhere; they bunged in a few rounds exactly the same exercise as we did before. We fanned out as far as we could to the wire and, oh, I must tell you one little incident. Just when these people were mortaring a big German got up out of the trench and he'd got a bandage round his head – he hadn't got a helmet on – and he started running zigzag backwards. And the chap next door to me got his rifle, I said, "Don't". For some reason or other, I don't know why, I said, "Don't". And I'm certain that that fellow started a panic, because when we went there these Prussian Guards, they put up their hands. And we captured about fifty of them again. And that was that. We got back to Ossy you see, and Ossy immediately sent 2 Company through us with Alfred Pollard. Alfred took his company through. Alfred was a terrific individualist, one of these fire-eating types and he went through and we passed bombs along to him and his company and he more or less left his company behind and just depended upon half a dozen stalwarts. And he bombed and he took two or three hundred yards of that trench right the way along. Alfred took them on and he really got them on the run. Then I had to extend my company out towards him because we were so thin on the ground again and he was right up at the danger end of things towards Oppy Wood, but by the evening we had taken all the ground which these battalions were supposed to have taken on the morning of the 28th.[18]

Pollard and Haine had between them retaken the strongpoint and all the trenches that were the objective of 1/RM and 7/Royal Fusiliers in the days before them, and what is more they held them. Pollard was an excellent bomber, very accurate and with a long range. He took on the

Germans and bombed them backwards up the front line by throwing bombs a long distance, and virtually single handedly took 1/RM's first objective from the day before. For this feat Pollard and Haine were awarded the Victoria Cross.

Second Lieutenant Alfred Oliver Pollard MC and Bar. DCM

On 29th April 1917 at Gavrelle, France, the troops of various units had become disorganised owing to the heavy casualties from shell fire and a subsequent determined attack with very strong forces caused further confusion and retirement. Second Lieutenant Pollard realised the seriousness of the situation and with only four men he started a counter attack with bombs, pressing it home until he had broken the enemy attack and regained all that had been lost and much ground in addition. This officer's splendid example inspired courage into every man who saw him.[19]

Second Lieutenant Reginald Lionel Haine.

On 28th/29th April 1917 near Gavrelle, France, when our troops were holding a salient which was being repeatedly counter attacked by the enemy. Second Lieutenant Haine organised and led six bombing attacks against a German strong point and captured the position, together with 50 prisoners and two machine guns. The enemy at once counter

Aerial photograph of the area north and west of Gavrelle, from the old German trenches to the Windmill. Where the annotation 'Marine' is marks the trenches where Lieutenants Pollard and Haine bombed their way up, both being awarded the VC for their actions.

'The Ditch', as seen from the 'Sunken Lane'. The authors estimate 'Downe's Drainpipe' to be between the second to fourth popular tree east of the Mayor's Garden.

attacked and regained the lost ground, but Second Lieutenant Haine formed a "block" in his trench and for the whole of the following night maintained his position. Next morning he again attacked and recaptured the position. His splendid example inspired his men during more than 30 hours of continuous fighting.[20]

The Pals of the 31st Division relieved the Royal Naval Division on the night of 29 April. Out of the Windmill trooped forty tired but determined Marines. Their achievement was one of the great, yet almost unknown, feat of arms in the history of the Royal Marines. For his leadership Lieutenant Newling was awarded the Military Cross. The fighting around Gavrelle had cost the RND in excess of 3000 men, now it would be the Pals turn.

1. Downe MM, Able Seaman LZ1828 RNVR, *In the Hell that was Gavrelle*, Published in Vol 28, *I was There,* Hammerton. London 1939. p1127-1131- This article is quoted as referring to the action of 23 April 1917. From the description of the participants and casualties, the action described actually refers to 28 April 1917. The first quote is incorrect as the sun would rise over Fresnes, not set.
2. War Diary, PRO ref WO95/3110.
3. Haine, R.L. Taped interview Imperial War Museum.
4. ibid
5. ibid
6. Falls, C. *Official History of the Great War Military Operations France and Belgium, 1917* vol 1 p425
7. Major C.E.C. Eagles was awarded the DSO for his work at Gavrelle. He was killed in action almost a year later during the Zeebrugge raid
8. Downe MM, Able Seaman LZ1828 RNVR, *In the Hell that was Gavrelle*
9. ibid
10. ibid-Able Seaman W.G.Willmer SZ112, of Chichester, Sussex, was killed in action on 28 April 1917.
10. Ibid.
11. Ibid.
12. Ibid. Able Seaman J.Singleton CZ1408 of Partick West was killed in action on 28 April 1917.
13. 188 Brigade War Diary WO95/3108.
14. ibid- my italics.
15. ibid- my italics
16. Trotman,H. Taped interview by Max Arthur
17. Haine,R.L. Taped interview Imperial War Museum
18. *London Gazette.* 8 June 1917
19. *London Gazette.* 8 June 1917

Chapter Four

ATTACKS AND TRENCH RAIDS

Pals attack on 3 May

Field Marshal Haig decided to continue the general advance in the Arras sector; the next attack was to be made on a very wide front on 3 May. 92 and 93 Brigade of the 31st Division was given the task of assaulting the enemy line in the Gavrelle sector. The 31st Division sector was to run from Oppy Wood to the end of the Sunken Road south of Gavrelle. The attack was to be in two halves, similar to that of the Royal Marines on 28 April. The reason for the two different phases was that those attacking on the Oppy side wanted to advance at a slower rate due to the broken and more hazardous terrain. Those attacking to the south wanted to advance much quicker as the ground was more open. These different speeds led to a complicated artillery schedule, with the potential danger that the faster attacking southern battalions would pull away from the northern battalions. The Windmill was the pivot in this action, and its possession was vital for the security of both attacks. The last potential problem was that the attacking units were totally unfamiliar with the ground over which they would be attacking, whilst the Germans knew the land and had planned its defence well. For this guide we will only be looking at 93 Brigade attack in front of Gavrelle.

On the night of 2 May the units moved into the jumping off line. The night was a bright one, with very full moonlight and the units coming downhill and entering the line were seen. The Germans opened a vicious artillery and machine-gun barrage, catching many of the attackers. Some men had to crawl over the bodies of their comrades to get into the jump off trenches. One of the communication trenches, Widow Trench, was so badly damaged that it had to be abandoned. The assaulting battalions of 93 Brigade were to be 15/West Yorks (1st Leeds), 16/WestYorks (2nd Leeds) and 18/West Yorks (2nd Bradford). In support were 18/DLI, who were put behind Gavrelle with two companies each side of the Arras Road so as to assist in either attack.

Northern Attack

The units involved in the northern attack were 16/West Yorks and 18/West Yorks. The northernmost border of their sector was Link Trench, which was about 300 yards to the south of Oppy Wood and

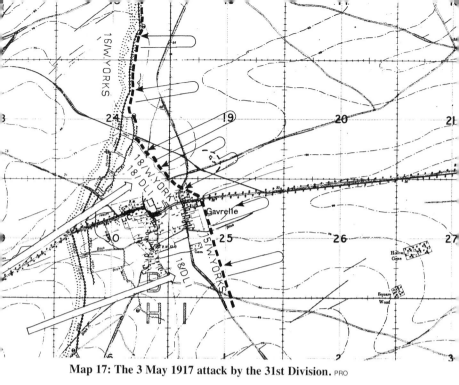

Map 17: The 3 May 1917 attack by the 31st Division. PRO

stretched to the Mayor's house in Gavrelle. Their objectives were firstly to take Windmill Trench then Windmill Support Trench. The attack commenced at 3.45am in semi-darkness with a mist. The effect of this, plus the gaps made in the assaulting battalions the night before, led to misdirection and confusion as men lost touch with each other. The advance went well to start with, but it soon became evident that the attack on Oppy Wood to the north, undertaken by other units of the 31st Division, had failed, as no friendly troops were seen. The Germans

No Man's Land. Looking west towards Gavrelle from the German Lines. The Mayor's House and Garden provided a strong position for the British troops, however, the exposed area east of Gavrelle made advances extremely costly.

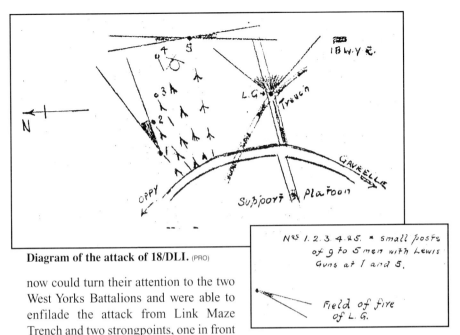

Diagram of the attack of 18/DLI. (PRO)

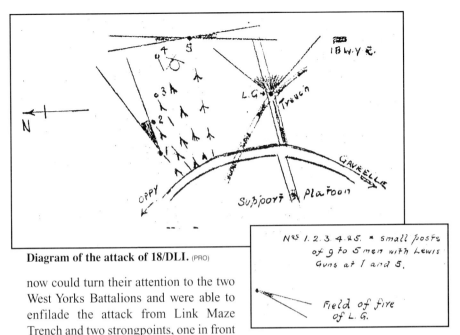

now could turn their attention to the two
West Yorks Battalions and were able to
enfilade the attack from Link Maze
Trench and two strongpoints, one in front
of the windmill and another in front of Gavrelle. The attackers were
literally mown down.

Counter attacks were developing from Oppy Wood and Link Maze,
similar to what overtook 1/RM a few days before. A Company of
18/DLI was sent for and originally it was planned to put them north of
the Railway line. Unfortunately, due to heavy machine gun fire, it was
decided to divert them to south of the railway and let the remnants of
16/West Yorks and 18/West Yorks filter back into that part of the line.
These parties, chiefly under Lieutenant- Colonel Croydon and Captain
Parker, bombed their way back to their old front line, taking some
prisoners with them. The attack on this part of the sector had failed,
and blocks were set up to stop the enemy from coming down the front
line from the north. This attack had cost these two units 160 fatalities,
with many more wounded or captured.

Southern Attack

In the south the assaulting force was 15/WestYorks. The Battalion
was starting from just in front and to the south east of Gavrelle. This
attack started at the same time as the northern attack but the advance
and artillery timetable were set at twice the rate (yards advance per
minute). This led to this attack getting well in front of the northern
attack and an alarming gap opening up between the two. Due to this,
the Battalion started to get enfiladed from its left by two strongpoints
which had not yet been dealt with by the units of the northern attack.

Due to the darkness and mist the advance went over a strongpoint without detecting it and its machine-guns and garrison fired into the rear of the Yorkshiremen. The attack was going well, many prisoners were being taken, but due to the German strongpoints the attack lost momentum. Many groups of prisoners, realising that there were no more British troops, turned on their captors and took them away with them. By 5.30am the attack had been defeated and the survivors retreated to their lines. The Germans, sensing a victory, counter attacked, but the artillery defeated them. The two companies of 18/DLI south of the Arras road were called forward. One company was put in the sunken lane to the south of Gavrelle and the other covered the north and north east of Gavrelle to link up with 18/West Yorks. Again, as on 28 April, a promising start ended in a fierce battle for survival. As the units to the north were fending off attacks from Oppy, 15/West Yorks were fighting off counter attacks from Railway Copse. The Battalion started the attack with 547 all ranks, but in a few hours had suffered 157 fatalities, 120 missing and 120 wounded. Again the wounded to dead ratio, normally three to one, was one to one, giving an indication of the vicious nature of the fighting in the battle of Arras. At 5.40am things had taken a turn for the worse, as word came through that the Germans had retaken the Windmill

Second Battle of Gavrelle Windmill.

The Windmill had been protected by two Stokes mortars and four Vickers machine-guns. Heavy shelling had killed the crews of these weapons and the Germans were able to move in on the wreckage during the failure of the attacks. It was imperative that the Windmill be retaken and C Company of 18/DLI was ordered to capture it at all costs. Second Lieutenant Hitchin DSO took an NCO with him and crept out and did some reconnaissance. The ground around the mill was bare and with no cover; there was a trench which lead out towards the Windmill from Gavrelle, but it was only deep for a short part, towards the mill it became very shallow and afforded no cover whatsoever. The reconnaissance revealed no obvious German activity. It was decided to take the Windmill in a frontal assault. There would be three waves, numbers nine and ten platoons in the first wave with eleven and twelve platoons in the second and third waves respectively. The attack would be made in three bounds: first bound from the starting trench to the road; second bound from the road to the railway; and lastly from the railway to the Windmill. At 6:45am the attack commenced. Immediately the Germans called down an SOS barrage.

The remains of Gavrelle Windmill.

The road was reached with no problem. The next bound was attempted but met with machine gun fire from three different directions, causing a withdrawal back to the road. Another attempt was made to get to the railway but was again driven off by severe machine-gun fire. Hitchin took personal charge of the attack and led another attempt which got to within fifty yards of the Windmill. The Germans surprisingly started to withdraw and were immediately shelled; unfortunately the shelling caused many casualties to the DLI and forced them to fallback to the road, having sustained fifty percent casualties. The DLI were now quite weak, and so Hitchin decided to attack the Windmill with small fighting patrols. The Germans had pulled back from the front of the Windmill, and slowly these patrols leap-frogged forward using shell holes and occupied the Windmill and ground around it. The process had taken four hours. The Germans still held one of the houses south of the windmill, but they were dislodged with rifle grenades. Snipers now started to bag large numbers of Germans who were trying to reinforce their comrades east of Gavrelle and those trying to retire from the Windmill. Hitchin patrolled around it and found the two Stokes mortars and four Vickers machine-guns and recovered them. The DLI had saved the day, the Windmill was once again in British hands having changed hands six times in the last couple of hours. It would remain in British hands for the next nine months. Reading accounts of the attacks of the 28 April and again on 3 May,[1] one thing stands out - the constant attention of the German air force. There were up to eight hostile aircraft over Gavrelle at any one

Able Seaman William Scott, (1891-1955) Hawke Battalion; 'B' Company, No. 5 Platoon, he was at Gavrelle during the capture in April, and was wounded by a shell on 3 June 1917, near Gavrelle.

time, strafing and bombing, giving testimony to the extent to which the RFC had been swept from the skies during 'Bloody April'.

Never a quiet sector

The attack on 3 May was a costly failure that achieved very little. It was the same down the whole of the line. This was effectively the end of the Arras offensive; although it spluttered on a little while longer in parts, it was never actively pursued in the Gavrelle sector. It would be wrong, however, to assume that the war had moved away from Gavrelle. On the contrary, Gavrelle was a very dangerous place to be. The Windmill position jutted out from the line, like a mini salient, and

was known as the Windmill Spur. Because it was exposed, to get to it was difficult; as one veteran commented it was almost certain death to move up to it in daylight. The Windmill was a constant target for shelling due to the fact that it became an excellent observation and sniping post. In the dead ground between the British lines and German lines were the fatalities of both sides from the actions on 28 April and 3 May. A veteran described this area as being like a butcher's shop, with bits of bodies lying everywhere and the smell was overpowering. He went on to say that this was the worst sector in which he ever served.[2]

Lieutenant-General Sir W Congreve VC, commanded XIII Corps, was wounded by shell fire on 12 June 1917 whilst making a customary visit to the Front Line at Gavrelle.

The RND served in this sector for the next couple of months, in partnership with the 31st Division. As stated, this was never a quiet sector whether in or out of the line. Pte Hubert Trotman of 2/RM describes an incident that took place on 26 May:

One day a chap had a large flat parcel come for him. He unwrapped it and it was a steel breast plate and a back plate with straps for the shoulders. We were due to go on a working party and we went off leaving the man and a friend with the breastplate. When we came back there was no sign of them in the trench, the breast plate was there though. We dug around and around and found them, both dead. They'd been killed by a shell. That was John Bull and Eric Coates, we buried them on the side of the road on the way to Arras. After that no one wanted to touch that breast plate.[3]

Raids and Attacks

Whilst casualties were relatively high from many causes commonly known as trench wastage, there were several notable incidents worth describing. These were raids and small scale attacks, carried out by

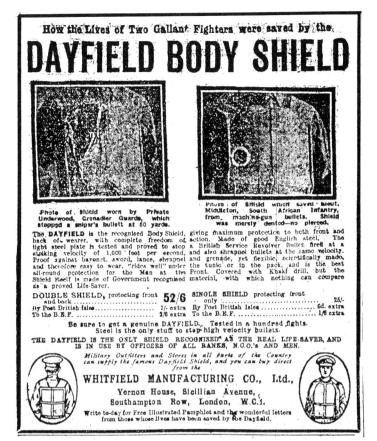
An advertisment in the newspapers for a bullet proof vest similar to that sent to Hubert Trotman's colleague.

both sides as part of normal trench routine. Raids were carried out for several reasons; to establish the identity of the unit opposite, to disrupt his routine and to try and maintain some sort of mental dominance over the enemy, as the British High Command believed in carrying the offensive forward at all times. The attacks were generally longer affairs designed to take and hold a piece of land, generally to improve a position. There is a significant difference between the two, and Gavrelle saw both types.

After the attacks of late April and early May things settled down a bit, but the British command still wanted to improve their positions. The grip on Gavrelle was rather tenuous, as it was still in a salient, and therefore threatened both from the north and the south. In June there were two attacks made, one on the northern and the other the southern part of the sector. These were designed to loosen the German grip around Gavrelle.

Attack on Charlie Trench

To the south of Gavrelle one of the original objectives of the April attacks, Greenland Hill, was still in German hands. It was quite a dominant feature, which gave the Germans good observation into Gavrelle and Roeux. The hill actually made a dent into the British front line. North of the hill the British front line ran from Gavrelle down Plouvain road for a few hundred yards and then bent back around the Greenland Hill; the Plouvain road continued through German lines and over the top of Greenland Hill. It was decided to take the line of trenches in front of Greenland Hill, on its western slope, which would loosen the German grip on it. The troops given the task of carrying out this attack were 102 (Tyneside Scottish) Brigade, which would be carried out in conjunction with units of 9th Division. The part played by the latter is outside the scope of this guide.

The objective of the attack was to take Charlie and Cupid trenches situated directly in front of the Tynesiders. On capturing these trenches, they were to advance to the German support lines, Cuthbert and Cod trenches, and establish a series of strongpoints. The date set for the assault was 5 June, the attack was to be on a three battalion front with 22/Northumberland Fusiliers on the left, 21/NF in the middle and 20/NF on the right; 23/NF would be the reserve. The Brigade would have a tremendous amount of artillery firepower at its disposal

See map page 87

consisting of 128 18pounders, thirty-eight 4.5 inch Howitzers and twelve 60 pounders, plus the Corps heavy artillery for counter battery work.

By 7.30pm the troops were in position and waiting. The Germans started shelling the front line at around 7.55pm, but stopped five minutes later. At that moment the offensive barrage opened and the Tynesiders advanced. The Germans initially put down a barrage on either flank of the Fusiliers, down the two main communication trenches, but switched the barrage onto the Gavrelle-Roeux road where it settled. On the left-hand side, the attack was met by heavy machine gun fire from Wit Trench to the northeast and this caused severe casualties to the 22/NF. However 22/NF got into their objective of Charlie Trench and inflicted severe casualties on the defenders. Several pockets of Germans were trapped in Charlie Trench and were dealt with by rifle grenades. This enabled 22/NF to gain touch with 21/NF on their right, and the whole of Charlie Trench was taken.

On the right of the sector the protective barrage opened up behind the German lines with the result that when the 20/NF attacked the defenders were able to machine-gun them unmolested. Nevertheless 20/NF got into their objective and heavy fighting ensued. The Fusiliers managed to take Curly Trench on their right and the end of Charlie Trench on their left, but a substantial party of Germans were

1/RMLI War Diary 12 September 1917: 'Bodies of Lieut N. Lion and 2nd Lieut Fielding previously reported missing – found and buried by battalion in front of Viscount Street, also eleven other ranks. According to official sources these bodies were buried at map reference B24 b 2.5.

After the war this area was combed for bodies. At B24 b 2.5 many graves were found that could be identified as RMLI only. These were buried in Orchard Dump Cemetery. One of the other ranks, Private Davies, is the only one of this group with a known grave at Orchard Dump. Above, two others of the eleven other ranks are pictured, Private Bettley (right) and Private Hampshire (left), both have no known grave.

sandwiched in between them. Although they had a party of the enemy in their position, 20/NF were in touch with the 21/NF on their left and units of 27 Brigade on their right, so were by no means isolated.

The next part of the plan involved establishing strong points in the German support lines in front of their objective. Six strongpoints were established as planned in Cod and Cuthbert trenches with little problem. At 11pm the northern-most post came under attack, which was beaten off. This post was attacked again at 2am on the 6th with much more determination. The enemy used grenades and trench mortars to try and take the strongpoint. This attack was defeated. Later, at 2.15am, the defenders of this post saw many Germans on the skyline coming at them from the direction of Wit Trench to the northeast. The defenders opened up with Lewis gun and rapid rifle fire and defeated the attack. The German force made several other advances with the same result and finally gave up at 3.40am. A lull followed and much frantic work started such as digging new communication trenches and putting out wire.

The lull continued into the afternoon of 6 June. It was decided to make a major effort to remove the Germans in Curly Trench. At 2pm a Stokes mortar was brought up and shelled the defenders and a frontal attack was put in by 20/NF. The Germans broke and ran but were met by Lewis gun fire in one of the strongpoints in Cod Trench and decided to surrender instead. These prisoners amounted to two officers, seventy-two other ranks, two light machine guns and one trench mortar. The whole of the objective had now been taken. When it got dark the Germans launched several attacks and got very close to success before being driven off. The northernmost strongpoint attracted the most attacks, and at one point the Germans captured it but

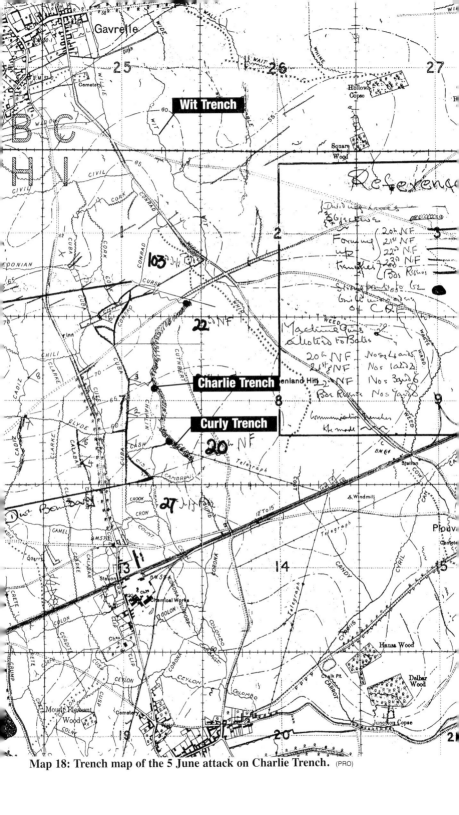

Map 18: Trench map of the 5 June attack on Charlie Trench. (PRO)

an immediate counter attack drove them out. When it became light it was evident that the enemy had suffered badly during these counter attacks, whilst several Germans trapped in shell holes and left behind surrendered. The success in holding off these counter attacks was put down to the presence of the strong points that had been put in front of the main lines of defence. These points broke up the attack before it had got to the defenders' main defence, operating with similar effect to the skirmish line of Napoleonic times. The Tynesiders were relieved during the night of the 7th/8th, having undertaken a successful operation.

Attack on Cordona Trench

An attack in the northern part of the Gavrelle sector on 28 June 1917 proved to be a complete contrast to the modern popular perception; it was highly successful, cost few casualties and produced tangible results. This type of attack was becoming popular at the time, small limited objectives that could be simply taken and held rather than the large all-out attacks popular earlier in the war.

The plan was simple. There was to be a limited attack which would involve the capture of Cordona Trench from the Windmill to Wood Alley Trench and from there to the junction of the German front line south of Oppy Wood. There was to be another attack by 5th Division units in conjunction with this, which would involve capturing the German front line in front of Oppy Wood, but this will not be covered in this guide. The idea of this attack was to make the Windmill less isolated, by securing the left flank of the Windmill. The 31st Division was entrusted with this task, and were given two weeks to plan and execute it. The preparations were started immediately. The communication trenches to Gavrelle were all in a shocking state and were not sufficient for the job. These were improved by the 1st Cavalry Division pioneers, whose work greatly contributed to the success of the operation. It would truly be an all arms effort. Saps were dug out into No Man's Land, and these would be joined with the captured trenches after the assault to form communication trenches. Another element in the success was the artillery support and preparation. The artillery fired on the whole Corps front evenly, not giving any clues to the focus of the attack. Certain trenches were given extra treatment, namely those that were thought to threaten the attacking troops. Wire cutting would start five days prior to the attack. Enemy batteries were spotted by air and registered by artillery units, and as many of the German batteries as possible would be engaged when the raid began. In order to give the troops assaulting Cordonna Trench better support, several batteries were pushed up close to the line in front of Bailleul. These would engage the usual routes which the enemy used to support his defence as well as support the infantry directly. Artillery was even cross-attached from the neighbouring Corps to assist the Cordonna Trench attack; they would lay down smoke and shrapnel. Four small raids were carried out on the Germans with mixed results in the days up to the operation but they confirmed that the extensive preparations were working.

The assaulting units were to be provided by 94 Brigade. The four battalions were assaulting on a three company front and from north to south the battalions were: 13/York and Lancs (1st Barnsley), 11/East Lancs (Accrington), 12/York and Lancs (Sheffield City) and 14/York and Lancs (2nd Barnsley). The Germans suspected something was up

Map 19: Trench Map showing the 28 June 1917 attack on Cordona Trench. (PRO)

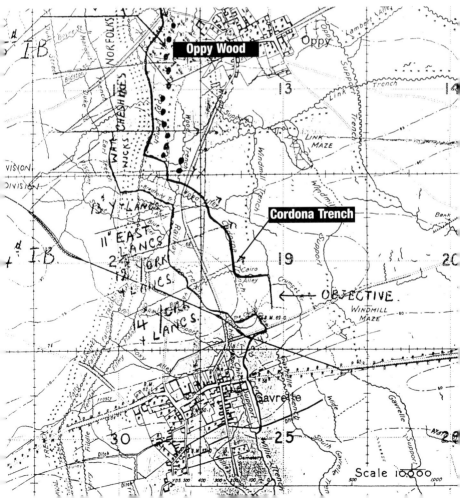

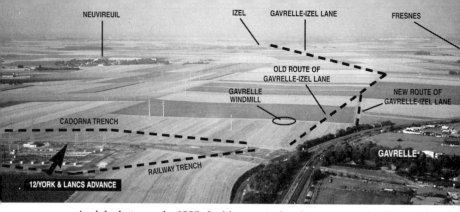

Labels on aerial photograph: NEUVIREUIL, IZEL, GAVRELLE-IZEL LANE, FRESNES, OLD ROUTE OF GAVRELLE-IZEL LANE, GAVRELLE WINDMILL, NEW ROUTE OF GAVRELLE-IZEL LANE, CADORNA TRENCH, GAVRELLE, RAILWAY TRENCH, 12/YORK & LANCS ADVANCE

Aerial photograph, 1998, looking east, showing area north of Gavrelle, with Railway and Cordona Trenches shown.

and put in more air patrols to try and observe what was going on and they even conducted a large barrage of the front line trench on the 27th. There were casualties, but it did not disrupt the operation.

The attack went in at 7:10pm on 28 June and was a great success; within minutes the objective was taken and consolidation started immediately. The success of this assault was due to the two weeks' preparation and planning, the speed at which the troops moved, the brilliant supporting barrage and the counter battery work. The casualties were extremely light with fatalities in single figures, whilst one battalion had no fatalities at all. On settling into their gains, the Pals were subjected to a violent thunderstorm, which made

Men of the York and Lancaster Regiment taking up wire for a night working party on the Oppy-Gavrelle sector. TAYLOR LIBRARY

consolidating their gains more difficult and hindered a German counter-attack. The Germans, though, had lost heavily, with their fatalities in the hundreds. This was a model attack, well planned, prepared and executed. More was achieved in this assault than in the bloody failure of 3 May. The Windmill Spur was now more secure, and the Germans' dominance from Oppy Wood was broken.

Raid on Gavrelle Trench 20 July 1917

The general perception of a raid is one of blackened faces, knuckle-dusters and coshes, launched at the dead of night. With a box barrage and a mad scramble they were carried out, often in total chaos, with many casualties sustained for the dubious knowledge of the identity of the unit opposite. There were many indeed like that, but not all, and Howe Battalion carried out a raid in the early hours of 20 July which was successful.

The area to be raided was Gavrelle Trench to the south of the Gavrelle-Fresnes road. The objective was to take a prisoner, inflict casualties and assess the conditions of the enemy trench. The raid was to be carried out by six officers and 180 other ranks (i.e. in company strength). The raid was rehearsed at least twelve times over five days. A box barrage was to be used; apart from the 63rd Divisional artillery, artillery support came from adjacent 17th and 5th Divisional artillery. Trench mortars were used on the flanks to help suppress the enemy machine guns. Twenty-one Vickers machine-guns were to be employed in covering this raid, which included guns from the adjacent units.

The raiders got into their positions at 12:40 am and the covering

Sketch of the raid by Howe Battalion on 20 July 1917. (From War Diaries, PRO).

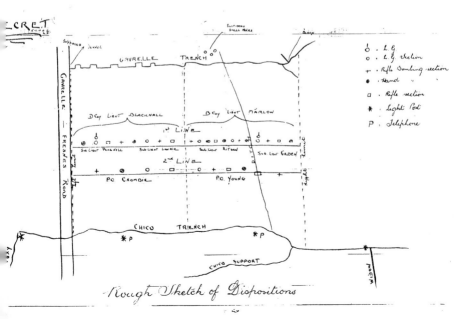

Map 20: Trench map showing the position of No Man's Land, from mid-1917 until the German March Offensive. During this nine month period Gavrelle Trench was raided many times. The Sap can be seen jutting into No Man's Land between the i and t in 'Ditch'.

barrages opened at 1am. The raid started and the German front line was entered on all points except for a twenty yard stretch which was protected by wire which was concealed in long grass and behind which the defenders held firm. Everywhere else the Germans ran and were either shot or ran into the box barrage. Prisoners were gathered and the raiders returned. The operation was completed in twenty minutes. In terms of casualties the raiders suffered seven

Oblique photograph of front line trenches east of Gavrelle. The sap and other features have been annotated. (IWM Q46116)

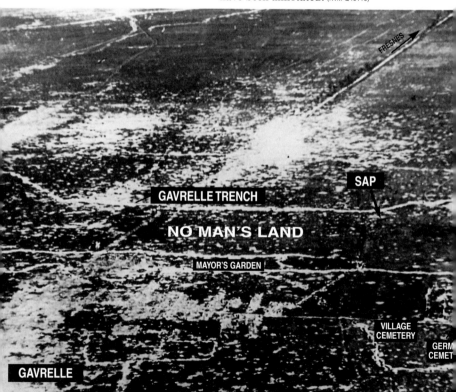

killed and seventeen wounded. They captured eleven prisoners of 128th Regiment, and estimated German losses were around twenty dead. It also discovered that the German trenches were four feet deep with a few funk holes, there were no dugouts, duckboards or sandbags – basically the German trench was in unusually poor repair. As an indication of the scale of support for this twenty-minute affair, the following figures were given in the post raid report. 800 trench mortar shells were fired and 32,000 machine gun rounds, which suppressed all hostile machine guns, and which resulted in the raid being conducted without interference. An interesting remark was made that, due to the high wind, trench mortar shells on the southern flank were blown onto the attackers that they were supposed to be protecting. Yet another lesson was learnt.

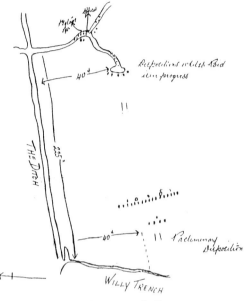

Sketch of the planned raid on the Sap by Anson Battalion on 7 September 1917. (PRO)

Raid on Gavrelle Trench 7 September 1917

Gavrelle Trench again was the subject of a raid on 7 September, this time the raiders were the Anson Battalion, and the objective, a small sap which was part of Gavrelle Trench. Again the raiders were given ample notice and managed to get ten practices in beforehand. The objective of the raid was simply to grab a prisoner. There was to be covering artillery, similar to the Howe raid, but this was to be on a much smaller scale, with just the Divisional artillery and light trench mortars contributing, whilst machine-gun cover was also to be provided. The size of the raiding party was also much smaller than the Howe raid, with just one officer and thirty men.

The raiders formed up at 9.35 pm and the barrage opened at 9.45pm. The raiders dashed out into No Man's Land and through the wire that had been well cut by the artillery. They jumped into the

Gavrelle trench to the south of the sap and landed almost on top of some Germans coming out of a dugout. One German ran and was shot, the other was grabbed. With their objective complete the raiders bundled their captive across No Man's Land and back into British lines. The raid lasted twelve minutes from start to finish. The cost to the raiders was one man killed and four wounded. The losses to the Germans were similar, with one prisoner taken from the 363rd Infantry Regiment of 214th Division. Again sound practice and accurate artillery led to success. This was to be the farewell to Gavrelle for the RND, the Division was posted to the Ypres Salient within days to join the Third Ypres offensive.

Raid on Gavrelle Trench 4 November 1917

47th Division

The area south of the Fresnes Road was again to attract a raid in early November. The raiders this time were to be Londoners from the 47th Division. This raid was going to be on a grander scale than those that had gone before. The raiders were to be from 23/London and 24/London regiments, each furnishing two companies, also there was to be a detachment of engineers from 520 Field Company. In total the number of raiders was 493 of all ranks, a sizeable force. The first target was to be Gavrelle Trench again, the second was to be the second line behind it, Crab, Cod and Crawl Trenches. The objective was again to grab prisoners, plus to kill as many of the enemy and destroy as much of his position as possible. Another difference in this raid was that it was to be a daylight one, timed to finish so that the men would be coming back as dusk settled with the setting sun in the Germans eyes.

The raid was practised over several days to perfect techniques and iron out any faults. For ten days prior to the raid, detachments of the raiding party were sent out into No Man's Land to patrol and become familiar with the ground over which they were to attack. Lanes were cut in the British wire, diagonal to the axis of the trench so that the gap could not be viewed from the front. The plan was that the raid was to start at 4.30 pm, with a barrage all the way down the line to help deceive the enemy. The raiders were to advance in two waves with each battalion forming each wave. The first wave was to take Gavrelle Trench, the second wave was to pass through and take the support line. The raiders were then to withdraw, with the second line first to withdraw. The total time for the raid was to be around thirty-five minutes. The date set for the raid was 4 November.

The troops gathered in the front line and, as planned, the original occupants (22/London) were withdrawn to make way for them. The

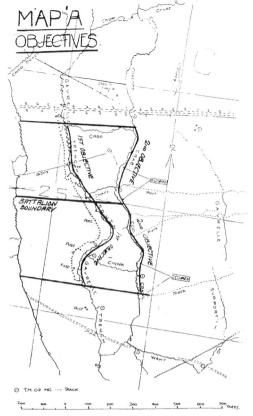

raid started on time with a creeping barrage that observers said was excellent and within four minutes the first wave was in the first objective. The enemy wire was well cut and did not hamper the advance, there was some opposition, but most of the occupants ran southwards down the trench or back into the protective British bombardment. The creeping barrage held there for a minute while a small advance in the barrage was made in the southern part of the sector where Gavrelle Trench ran back a bit to allow that part of the trench to be crept up upon. The barrage then lifted and the second wave filtered through and onto the second objective. Now there was some opposition, for at the junction of Gavrelle Trench and Carp Trench (communication trench), a group of Germans made a stand. These were bombed back down Carp Trench and were all killed. The

Objectives and battalion boundaries of Trench raid by the 47th Division, on 4 November 1917. Sites of trench mortars and machine guns are indicated. (PRO)

second objective was reached after twelve minutes. The opposition again ran either south or back into the British barrage. The only opposition was again in the area of Carp Trench, where it joined Crab Trench. The Germans here stood their ground but surrendered when their officer was killed.

The raiders now embarked on their mission of destruction, all war material was thrown into dugouts and the engineers blew these up. It was found that at the top of Crab trench there was a tunnel under the Fresnes road which could hold a platoon and allow reinforcements to come from the north of the road. The engineers tried to blow this tunnel up but failed, but it was rendered useless for the course of this action. Other tunnels under the road were suspected but not found. Bodies and trench material were booby trapped by leaving grenades with pins out under these objects. Thirty-five minutes after the start of the raid the

95

second wave started back to Gavrelle Trench, filtered through it and back to the British wire. Gaps in the wire had been marked with large white discs. After the second wave had passed, the first wave withdrew taking trophies and prisoners, with a Lewis gun crew to cover any German counter attack. The white discs were removed and the Lewis gun team withdrew. It was all over in forty-five minutes.

The outcome of the raid was that fifteen prisoners of the 459th Regiment of 236th Division were taken along with five light machine guns, one trench mortar and much other equipment. The losses to the raiders amounted to four other ranks killed with thirty one wounded. The Germans retaliated by shelling the British front line which had just been re-occupied by 22/London, who lost nine killed and four wounded. It was ironic that their fatalities were larger than those units taking part in the raid. This was termed a successful raid; from a prisoner they found that they were ordered if attacked to vacate the front line, which accounts for the enemy response to the raids. The Germans regarded the Fresnes Line as being the more important and they were working hard on it. The German losses were very heavy and amounted to around a hundred killed. The large number of casualties was due in part to the fact that there was a working party out at the time which got caught in the artillery attack.

1. Various war diaries mention the German air force machine gunning the British troops with a demoralising effect.
2. Gibson, R and Oldfield, P. *Sheffield City Battalion,* Barnsley 1988 p190
3. Trotman, H. Taped interview with Max Arthur. Privates Bull and Coate are buried beside the Arras road in Point-du-Jour Military Cemetery, Plot I, Row F Graves six and seven

The wreckage of a German gun outside Gavrelle, 27 June 1917. TAYLOR LIBRARY

Chapter Five

1918

56th Division takes over the Line

In February 1918 another London Territorial Division, the 56th, took over the Gavrelle sector from the 62nd Division. The sector stretched from just south of Oppy Wood in the north, to 500 yards south of Gavrelle. The 56th Division went to France in February 1916 and had its first major action on the Western Front at Gommecourt on 1 July, going on to fight in the rest of the Somme battles. The Division then took part in the Battle of Arras, including operations on the Scarpe on 3 May. It then got transferred to Ypres and fought around Langemarck, and was then moved south and took part in the Cambrai offensive. Since its introduction to the Western front, the 56th Division had fought in alost every major offensive planned and carried out, and was about to take part in the largest defensive battle of its short existence.

Since the Russians had capitulated it was long known that an offensive by the Germans was planned to knock the allies out of the war before The United States could mobilise in numbers. The question was where and when this attack would take place. Part of normal

A trench block. These trench blocks were placed in trenches, especially communication trenches, to impede the attacking enemy. The block could quickly be brought down. Some trench blocks were wooden swing doors. Once consolidated the 'block' would be reinforced with sandbags and loop holes would be made to fire through.

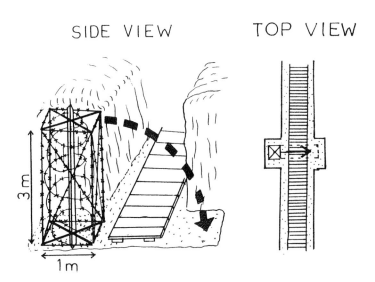

SIDE VIEW   TOP VIEW

3 m

1m

routine was to raid the enemy trenches to take a prisoner to identify the unit opposite and extract information. A raid was carried out on 9 March by 13/London (Kensington) which was highly successful and in which four prisoners had been taken. On interrogation it was revealed that an offensive was imminent. This led to a heightened state of alert, stand to earlier in the morning, and artillery shoots on areas of concentration and communication.

5/London (London Rifle Brigade) raided the German trenches on 16 March, but got caught up on the wire. They did manage to get in and kill some Germans, but took no prisoners. The information they did gain was that the enemy front line was strongly held. On 19 March the 56th Division changed the organisation of units holding the front line from a three-brigade front to a two-brigade front. The rest of the Gavrelle story as regards the 56th Division is concerned with 169 Brigade, who was holding Gavrelle itself.

Preparations for defence.

The nature of the defences of Gavrelle were different to those at the time of its capture in 1917; whilst the methods of attack and defence had changed also. The front line now consisted of a series of defended localities, or posts. The distance between these posts varied by as much

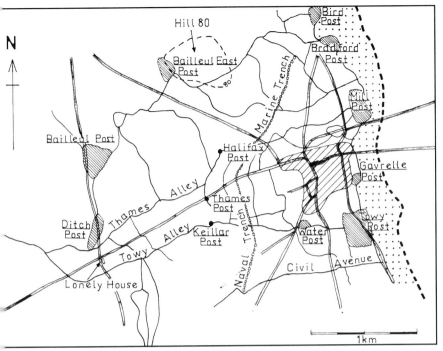

Map 22: The new strongpoint post defence system at Gavrelle.

as 800 yards; these gaps were defended by artillery and machine gun fire from the rear, and by interlocking machine gun fire from these posts. They were garrisoned in strengths varying from a platoon to a company. The names of the posts in the sector held by 169 Brigade were, from north to south: Bird, Bradford, Mill, Gavrelle and Towy , named after nearby trenches or features. This series of posts was not designed to be held for long, as it was intended that the garrisons would fight a short action then withdraw to the second line of defence.

This second line of defence was 800 yards behind the posts and was known as the Naval Marine line. It consisted of a single line of trench, which consisted of Naval Trench and Marine Trench, which ran from north to south. The wire in front of these trenches had been much strengthened of late by the London battalions.

The third line of defence, which lay 1000 yards behind the front line, was a stronger defensive position. This was the Bailleul-Willerval Line (Red Line). It consisted of good, well wired and protected trenches, with a series of strong posts included in the line. In 169 Brigade's sector there were three strong posts, from north to south they were: Bailleul East, Bailleul Post and Ditch Post. The Naval-Marine line was linked to the Red Line by a series of communication trenches called Towy, Thames, North Tyne and Tyne Alleys. These gave evacuation routes from the Naval Marine Line to the Red Line.

The Forth and final defensive line was the Point du Jour-Thelus line, which was 1500 yards behind the front line. This was a good trench system with two large defended posted in this sector, Point du Jour Redoubt and Railway Post. There was another line slightly in front of this position, on the northern half of the sector, called the Farbus line. The real advantage of this last area of the Point du Jour was the fact that the observation was superb, the whole of the front was under observation and therefore artillery could be directed better.

German Offensive Starts

On 21 March the Germans attacked south of the River Scarpe, mainly on the Somme front, and made good progress against the British Fifth Army. In Gavrelle the only sign of enemy action was an increase in air activity and behind the lines movement. However the wire in front was mortared to break up the wire and Towy Post was shelled. Things were afoot, and on the 23rd, at 5:30pm, a mine was exploded under the wire of Towy Post.

The following day a wounded German stated that there were fresh divisions from the eastern front opposite and that they would attack on the 26th. The attack would have its right flank on Oppy, the Germans would advance 4000 metres and then swing right towards Vimy, and deliver a left hook to Vimy Ridge. Interrogation of prisoners revealed that there were sixty trench mortars opposite and this number was

German storm troopers in action.

Aerial photograph of north-east Gavrelle looking south-west, taken in 1987, a few years after the by-pass was constructed, showing the old Gavrelle to Oppy road.

rising. On the night of the 25th an inter-battalion relief went on, with the 16/London relieving the 2/London on the right hand sector of the brigade line. On relieving Gavrelle Post, it was found that the post was empty, the occupants gone, there were signs of a struggle and two bodies, but no sign of the others. It can be presumed that there had

Vast numbers of heavy guns were brought up by the Germans: effective use of artillery would be the ultimate war winner.

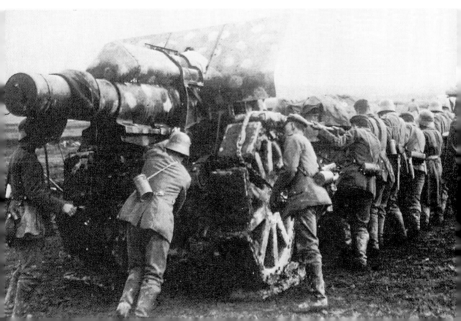

been a raid and the garrison taken away. On the 27th there were further changes to the 56th divisional responsibilities. It was ordered to take over the frontage of the 3rd Canadian Division at Tommy and Arleux Posts on the northern boundary. Although not within the scope of this study, the effect of this move was to stretch out 169 Brigade thinner as each brigade in the front line spread out a bit more to take over the Canadian positions. So on the night of 27 April, 169 Brigade was dispersed in the following way:

16/London was occupying the Towy Post with one company, the rest were in the Naval Marine line; 5/London was occupying Mill, Bradford and Bird Posts with part of its strength in the Naval Marine line; 2/London was in the Bailleul-Willerval line; one company of 1/5 Cheshires (Pioneers) were in the Farbus line. In Reserve were a detachment of 176th Tunnelling Company in the Point du Jour redoubt, and two companies of 1/London from 167 Brigade in reserve behind this.

The changes had barely been finished when the German offensive started. During the night of 27/28 March gas shells started falling around the Brigade headquarters, artillery positions and the trenches. At around 3am a violent bombardment started on the trenches concentrating on the Red line and the Thelus-Point du Jour line. At 5am the barrage moved off these rear areas onto the Naval Marine line, and an extremely violent bombardment was opened on the front line posts.

5/London Sector

At Mill Post the garrison was virtually wiped out by the bombardment, one survivor staggered into the battalion headquarters reporting that all the trenches and dugouts were blown in and the garrison with it. The enemy attacked in large numbers and overran the blown in remains of the posts and swarmed up to the Naval Marine line. The battalion headquarters, which was in Marine Trench, suddenly found itself in the front line. The Germans came on in three large attacks, but was severely hampered by the wire, which had been recently erected. This delay in the wire allowed the defenders to shoot down many of the enemy. However, they seemed abundant, and the number of defenders dwindling; the Germans managed to get into the Marine Trench system and outflank the Londoners. Lieutenant Colonel Hussey, the commanding officer of 5/London, ordered his men to withdraw southwards down Marine Trench to the junction of Thames Alley. They managed this and continued a fighting withdrawal down

```
                    ┌─────────────────┐
                    │   169 BRIGADE   │
                    └─────────────────┘
          ┌──────────────────┼──────────────────┐
┌───────────────────┐ ┌───────────────────┐ ┌───────────────────┐
│    16TH LONDON    │ │    5TH LONDON     │ │    2ND LONDON     │
│(QUEEN'S WESTMINSTER│ │(LONDON RIFLE      │ │ (ROYAL FUSILIERS) │
│     RIFLES)       │ │    BRIGADE)       │ │                   │
└───────────────────┘ └───────────────────┘ └───────────────────┘
```

Structure of 169th Brigade.

Thames Alley until they reached the Red Line, in which they spread out, setting up headquarters in Bailleul Post and prepared themselves for the next assault. It was still only 10.30am.

16/London

In the south the story was similar. At 7:15am the Germans moved against the front line. Towy Post was attacked and Captain Lownes and the remains of his B Company were quickly forced into the support line. The Germans swept through Gavrelle village, their advance being described as 'shoulder to shoulder'. By 7.30am the situation at Towy Post was desperate, the Germans had gone past on both flanks, and the front line trench system had also been taken. To make matters worse the Germans were bombing up Towy Alley behind the post. The effect of the Germans taking Gavrelle and advancing was to drive a wedge between the 5th and 16th Londons. Lownes and his men now came out of the rear of Towy Post, as there was no future in trying to hold it. They bombed back down Towy Alley, through the advancing Germans and made it to the Naval Line to rejoin the rest of the battalion. The Battalion made a stand here and inflicted serious casualties, so that there was a chance that this line could be held. Likewise, with the 5/London line, the Germans managed to break in, as their numbers began to tell. Where 5/London had vacated their part of Marine Trench, the Germans were coming down from the north; but they had also got in to the south. The Westminsters were hemmed in against the Gavrelle road, whilst the Germans were held back by blocks in the trenches. The position was untenable and it was decided to make a fighting retreat down Thames Alley to the Red Line. There was an unfortunate incident in which a block in a trench that was holding back the Germans was destroyed by British artillery, letting in the Germans, and the Westminsters in that trench were all killed. The remaining Westminsters managed to conduct a fighting retreat back down the Thames Alley and joined the other battalions in the Red Line.

What these battalions had achieved was remarkable. They had inflicted heavy casualties. They had conducted a controlled fighting withdrawal to a better position, which was a very skilled manoeuvre to

British dead in a communication trench, March 1918.

conduct, marked by the fact that it was a fighting withdrawal. The battalions were dispersed in the Red Line as follows: 5/London holding the northern sector with its headquarters in Bailleul Post; 2/London in the central portion with its headquarters in Ditch Post; lastly 16/London in the southern sector. 16/London and 5/London held portions of Towy and Thames alleys with blocks holding back the Germans. It was decided to blow in the thirty yards of both these trenches closest to the enemy to deny their use to the Germans. The Germans made tentative attacks but failed to get the break in the line that they had hoped for. The rest of the afternoon the Red Line was subjected to heavy shelling and low level strafing by German planes. The line held, but for the first time in nearly a year Gavrelle was in German hands. This was to be the high water mark, though, and the Germans advanced no further in this sector. Today a demarcation stone marks this spot.

South of Gavrelle

Adjoining the 56th Division to the south was the 4th Division. The scope of this guide only covers 12 Brigade's sector which joined 56th Division a few yards to the south of Towy Post. The defensive system in this sector was similar to that of the 56th Division. In the front line there was 2/Essex in Charlie Trench, which was a continuation of 16/London's line. The next line of defence was a continuation of the Naval Marine line. This line, instead of running north to south, ran north east to south west as it ran down to the River Scarpe behind Fampoux. In this line was 2/Lancashire Fusiliers, whose position was in the shape of a St.Andrew's cross. They were disposed as follows: on one arm, in Civil Ave and Humid Trench, was A Company under Second Lieutenant Cassidy; this position stuck out from the rest of the line. To their south west was D Company in Harry and Hussar trenches, and to their right was a part of B Company in Hudson Trench. On the other arm the rest of the battalion was aligned in a north west to south east direction. C Company was in Trent Trench, which was a continuation of the Bailleul-Willerval Line, which crossed the trenches in front at the junction of Hudson and Hussar trenches. In Hyderabad Trench was the rest of B Company. The final line was Effie and Elba trenches, these were a continuation of the Point du Jour lines, and in occupation were 1/KORL plus some pioneers and engineers. Since the Germans offensive had started ground had been lost south of the Scarpe and preparations had been made to withdraw troops to the line currently occupied by 2/Lancashire Fusiliers. Consequently the ground had been reconnoitred carefully, and artillery and other support services had been thinned out and pulled back in preparation for withdrawal.

See map page111

A Victoria Cross for the Lancashire Fusiliers.

At 3am the Germans bombardment started on 2/Essex, and at 6.30am the Germans were seen cutting the wire and their attack started. The Germans attacked in packed ranks and the Essex men took a heavy toll of them. Their resistance was ended when, under the cover of mist, the Germans infiltrated south of Towy Post past their left flank and in behind them. At 9am just the commanding officer and fifty men were able to escape back to the Fusiliers line at Hudson Trench as their comrades were buried under the sheer weight of the German onslaught. The Fusiliers now braced themselves for their turn, their instructions were not to give an inch, and any territory wrested from them would be at a very high price. There was some concern that the right flank was at risk, so C Company 1/KORL was bought forward to Hyderabad Trench to reinforce B Company 2/Lancashire Fusiliers. The Germans regrouped and launched their attacks down the communication trenches, which led from the front line to the Fusiliers position. These were Chili, Civil and Caledonian alleys, which ran parallel to Towy and Thames alleys. The Germans attacks only made headway in one area, at 10am they had got into the junction of Harry and Humid trenches. This effectively cut off A Company from D Company and isolated them. D Company erected blocks and barricades in Hussar Trench, and after hand to hand fighting held off the Germans. A Company, though, suffered serious casualties, their supply of bombs and ammunition were nearly exhausted. The Germans had already got past their right and it now appeared that they had got past their left as well and now they were virtually surrounded. There was only one way in which they could possibly escape, that was over the open ground and back to Trent Trench, which was a daring and potentially hazardous manoeuvre. Second Lieutenant Cassidy ran up and down the trench encouraging his men as it became clear that they were actually making a last stand in Humid trench. Only six survivors of A Company made it back to their colleagues, Cassidy and the rest were killed where they stood. This stand probably saved the 4th Division, as it saved their left flank. For his outstanding feat Cassidy was awarded a posthumous Victoria Cross.

Second Lieutenant
Lieutenant
Cassidy VC

Second Lieutenant Bernard Mathew Cassidy. Second Battalion Lancashire Fusiliers

On 28 March 1918 at Arras, France, at a time when the flank of the division was in danger, Second Lieutenant Cassidy was in command of the left company of his battalion. He had been given orders to hold on to the position at all costs and he carried out this instruction to the letter. Although the enemy came in overwhelming numbers he continued to rally and encourage his men, under terrific bombardment, until the company was eventually surrounded and he was killed.[1]

Second Lieutenant Cassidy's body was not identified after the war, and he is commemorated on the Arras Memorial.

Death of an artist and poet

During the rest of the 28th the Germans made numerous attacks on Hussar Trench, but these were beaten off with Lewis guns and personal bravery, and the defenders even carried out some counter attacks. During the afternoon the Fusiliers were reinforced by the divisional reserve, this was the 10% of every unit that was kept back for reserve purposes, which was now being moved forward to support the Fusiliers. After dark the Germans made several attacks on Hyderabad Trench, but were beaten off. The Fusiliers, though, lost touch with 11 Brigade to the south and the Germans got in between, but 1/Rifle Brigade were bought forward and ejected them and regained touch between the two brigades. South of the Scarpe ground had been lost, which left the units north of the Scarpe in a dangerous position. 11 Brigade was compelled to fall back, which meant that 12 Brigade had to do the same to conform. The Fusiliers pulled back a bit during the night of 28/29th. B Company and C Company 1/KORL were now in Hudson Alley and Stoke Trench, D company were also in Stoke Trench, C

The artist and poet Isaac Rosenberg, killed 1 April 1918, south-west of Gavrelle.

company and the remnants of 2/Essex were in Trent Trench. The trenches were blocked and barricaded at the likely entry points. At dawn the Germans made several half-hearted attacks but were again seen off with no ground lost. At 9am the Germans launched several bombing attacks; things were now getting difficult for the Fusiliers as their supply of bombs and ammunition was getting very low, but they still held their ground. The attacks stopped now and remained stable for the rest of the 29th and the 30th. During the night of 30/31 March 1/KORL relieved the Fusiliers.

During the days of 31 March and 1 April the Germans made no attempt to attack, but they did bombard the Lancasters with artillery. Things changed in the early hours of 2 April, as the war diary explains:

> *About 5-45 am a party of the enemy, about 200 strong raided, our front line. A determined attack was made by the enemy, bringing with him packs, barbed wire and other material as if sure of occupying the trench. He was ejected with loss, leaving in one trench 7 dead and two wounded after about an hour's fighting. Our casualties were Second Lieutenant R.Frame killed and 50 ORs wounded.*[2]

Killed in the above engagement was artist and poet Isaac Rosenberg. What happened to him exactly is uncertain, and the subject of much speculation. His date of death officially is 1 April 1918, but the war diary gives the only significant action as that quoted above.

A Victoria Cross for the Canadians.

The Canadians relieved the 4th Division on 8 April. The Canadians had been spared the ordeal of the German offensive up to this point, but were now being drawn into the action. It would not be long before they made an impact in their customary style. It was decided that 14/Canadian Battalion would raid the Germans opposite on the night of 27 April.

The objective of the raid was to get some prisoners, destroy enemy war materials and to exert some moral superiority over the Germans. The raiders were divided into six parties, A to F, plus a Lewis gun section. Each of these parties were to be led by a lieutenant and consisted of twenty-five men, whilst an NCO led the Lewis gun section. The objectives of the parties were as follows:

A & B were to follow the barrage, and eliminate the listening posts. When the barrage was past the enemy trench the two parties were to enter the enemy trench. 'A' group was to turn south, clear the trench, and form a block for the Lewis gun team to defend with bombers. 'B' group was to work north and clear the trench. C group was to wait behind A and B and support A and B if necessary. After the success of A and B's mission, C group was to escort prisoners back from all other

There was little time to bury the dead on the battlefield. Bodies were often marked by comrades to help collection after. Here a rifle has been put into the ground to mark the body.

108

groups involved in the raid. D group was to follow the barrage along Cable Trench, take a known enemy post, occupy it, block the trench and defend it with bombs. E group was to push up Hussar Trench and eliminate two blocks in it. F groups were to push along Cable Trench behind D group. Once D had performed its task, F would pass in front of it, form a block and install a Lewis gun and mop up along Hoary Trench. The raiders were warned not to take any identification discs or shoulder titles into action; many years later this could have implications on the identification of bodies found on the field. An interesting warning was given to the raiders that, in the event of capture they were only obliged to give name, rank and number, but were warned about stool pigeon tricks. This was when a German in British uniform was put amongst prisoners to gain their confidence hoping that they would let secrets slip to a 'comrade'. It was, apparently, a common German tactic.

The raiders were to be in position by 12.45 am of 27 April. This was achieved with no problem. By 12.50 am, they were ready to go. The supporting creeping barrage opened at 01.00am. The raiders advanced at 01.01am. behind a perfect barrage, A and B groups following it closely. A group got into the German trench and encountered stiff opposition. This was mainly due to the personal bravery of an officer. He was shot and the enemy lost the will to fight on. Prisoners were taken, but some Germans were in the dugouts and refused to come out, so the dugouts were blown in, entombing the occupants. The Lewis gun section set up a block after killing the Germans in the way. The enemy attempted a counter attack, and were allowed to get close to the raiders. The raiders then showered them with bombs and bayoneted the survivors whilst they were still stunned. B group got into the German trenches and met some opposition, who were bayoneted. The defenders attempted to get a machine gun up onto the parapet, but the crew were stunned by a well-aimed rifle grenade and the survivors bayoneted. C group, who was there to support A and B, was not needed for that purpose and decided to pitch into the nearest fighting. D group met some opposition at the first of the blocks that they were to capture, but they overcame it and went on to the second block, overcame it in turn and took the machine-gun guarding it. E group encountered the hardest fighting. The Germans in Hussar Trench were hemmed in by a box barrage, and were left with only two options, surrender or fight; they chose to fight. The fought very well and held up the attack. Lieutenant McKean, E group's officer, sent back to the Canadian lines for more grenades three times. The attack was still stalled, Lieutenant McKean decided to end it. He got out of the trench and jumped over the German block, headbutting the German defender whom he then finished off with a revolver. A German attempted to bayonet him and he was shot also. The rest of McKean's men followed him over and they moved on to take another block. The Germans here also fought for a while and then ran for shelter in a dugout. This dugout was blown in by a charge laid by Sergeant Jones, who unfortunately was also killed by the blast. F party advanced on time but were held up by wire, and the Germans pelted them with bombs. The Canadians were not to be denied and jumped over the wire and bayoneted the defenders. They captured the rest of their objective, taking a 'pineapple' thrower. The parties withdrew without much retaliation and made it back to Canadian lines. The raid had taken just over forty-five minutes. Canadian losses were two killed and eleven wounded. They had taken twenty-six prisoners, two of whom died from wounds soon after capture, and it was estimated that total German losses in the raid were around forty.

This raid was a success at a time where things were very difficult for the allied forces. It must have come as a huge shock to the Germans to be raided in such a manner by a 'defeated' enemy. The reason why this raid succeeded was due to the attitude of all those who took part. The other ranks were resolute in their approach. Their artillery protection was described as perfect. Their officers set a fearless example of leading from the front and all personally killed a few defenders each. One officer in particular stood out, Lieutenant McKean, who was awarded the Victoria Cross. This Victoria Cross was won only yards away from where Cassidy won his Victoria Cross the month before.

German prisoners being searched. TAYLOR LIBRARY

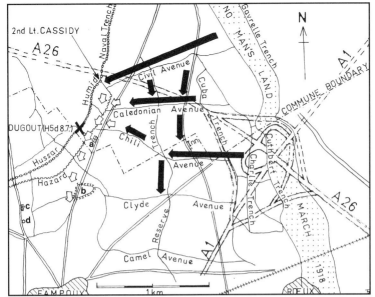

Map 23: German 28 March 1918 attack south of Gavrelle. The Germans quickly overwhelmed the Front Line, but the British held the Reserve Trench, forcing the Germans to attack along the communication trenches. The site of Cassidy's stand is indicated. This allowed the troops to retreat and regroup further south at Hyderabad Redoubt. The autoroutes have been superimposed to help present day orientation. Note the position of Cuthbert and Charlie Trenches. Also plotted is the Dugout that McKean VC attacked a month later.

a = Site of Chili Trench Cemetery
b = Hyderabad Redoubt
c = Site of Sunken Road Cemetery
d = Site of Celtic Cross Memorial

Lieutenant George Burdon McKean 14th Batttalion, C.E.F.

On 27/28 April 1918 at the Gavrelle sector, France, when Lieutenant McKean's party was held up at a block in the communication trench by intense fire, he ran into the open, leaping over the block head first on top of one of the enemy. Whilst lying there, he was attacked by another with a fixed bayonet. He shot both of these men, captured the position, then sent back for more bombs, and until they arrived he engaged the enemy single-handed. He then rushed a second block, killing two of the enemy, capturing four others, and driving the remainder into a dugout, which he then destroyed.[3]

Lieutenant George McKean, VC, 14/Canadian. (NAC PA2716)

111

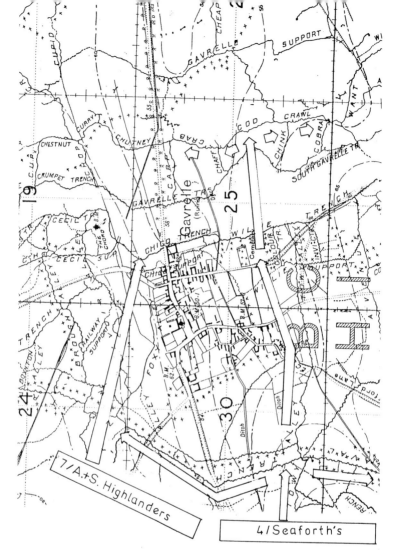

Map 24: The advance of the 51st Division 26 August 1918.

August 1918, Gavrelle recaptured.

In August 1918 the British army, after months of determined defence, turned on the Germans. To the south the offensive had been in full swing since 8 August with the start of the '100 Days' uninterrupted

The ruins of the Mayor's House. (Henri Lequette)

advance. It was not until the end of August that Gavrelle was liberated, this time by the Scottish Territorials of the 51st (Highland) Division. The manner of the recapture of Gavrelle was very different to the events of April 1917. During August the front had been pushed closer and closer to Gavrelle, and by the 25th it was a few hundred yards short, with an advanced post as close as the junction of Marine Trench and Towy Alley. In the early hours of 26 August the Germans assaulted this advanced post and drove out the Scotsmen, but they recovered this position a few hours later at 6am. At 10.45am activity was seen in Gavrelle with the enemy seen moving down the Gavrelle-Fresnes road; it appeared that the Germans were retreating to defend the Fresnes line. At 11.30am, 8th Division, to the north, pushed up to Railway Trench, and the 4/Seaforths patrolled up Marine Trench and Thames Alley. At 12 noon, 4/Seaforths and 7/Argylls were ordered to establish posts up the length of Marine Trench from east of Gavrelle to Viscount Street. By 5pm this had been done, with 4/Seaforths establishing posts from Towy Alley along Marine Trench up to Thames Alley, whilst 7/Argylls patrolled from there up to and into Tyne Alley. During the night of 26/27 August patrols of 7/Argylls continued their consolidation of Marine Trench, on their right patrols of 4/Seaforths pushed forward to the south of Gavrelle and established posts in Cod and Crab Trenches. At 5am 4/Seaforths found Willy Trench unoccupied and therefore occupied it, and then extended up Foxy Alley and joined up with 7/Argylls at Chico Trench. Gavrelle had been encircled and recaptured at minimal cost. The Germans made a small counter attack at 5pm. A patrol of sixty attacked and pushed the Scotsmen out of the Windmill and the posts at Cod and Crab Trench. These posts were regained by 4/Seaforths, though after a stiff fight, and the area was now secure. Units of the 8th Division, which extended their line southwards, relieved the Scotsmen. The Scotsmen had suffered just eight killed. Gavrelle was now liberated until another war spread across France just over twenty years later.

1. *London Gazette* Date for VC, 3 May 1918.
2. War Diary 1/KORL, PRO ref WO95/1506.
3. *London Gazette* Date for VC, 3 May 1918

A sketch of Gavrelle which appeared in *Mudhook*, the trench magazine of the RND. It shows the crucifix from the civilian cemetery, which was a well known feature. Note how overgrown the area was.

Chapter Six

AFTER THE ARMISTICE

At the end of the war the rural village of Gavrelle was nothing but rubble. The fields of the commune were pock-marked with shell holes and criss-crossed with trenches. There was a gaping hole of a crater to the south where a mine had been blown, under the strongpoint of Towy Post. Everywhere, isolated and in clusters, were the graves of hundreds of the fallen.

Slowly most of the residents came back to the ruined village to start rebuilding. Back in Britain the British League of Help put out a plea for municipalities to adopt a town or village destroyed on the Western Front, and help with its construction. Most urgently needed were the construction of public buildings, school furniture, and agricultural equipment. Since the Queen's Westminster Rifles were at Gavrelle in 1918, the council of the City of Westminster voted to adopt Gavrelle and help with the reconstruction[1].

Before this could commence, Gavrelle had to be cleared of battlefield debris. In Vitry-en-Artois, there was a prisoner of war camp, No. 306[2]. The Germans in this camp were 'employed' to clear the battlefield. Unexploded shells and ammunition were collected and disposed of. The corkscrew pickets and barbed wire were collected for their scrap metal or to be recycled. The wood was urgently needed for fuel and to provide temporary housing for returning villagers. Wood was also needed as pit props to help get the Lens coalfields back into

German prisoners of war clearing the eastern Arras battlefield early 1919. They came from the PoW camp No. 306 at Vitry-en-Artois. (IWM Q49586)

The ruins of Gavrelle. (NAC PA4604)

production; however the mines were badly damaged and coal was not produced until 1921. This stripping of the wood resulted in the rapid collapse of many of the famous strongpoints and dugouts in the area.

Besides the clearing of battlefield debris, the commune was also scattered with graves, isolated and in clusters. The two clusters with over forty graves were left as war cemeteries, they are Naval Trench Cemetery and Chili Trench Cemetery. All the other graves which were found were taken into concentration cemeteries in the area. Some of the graves had crosses to mark them, but many of the crosses were destroyed in the fighting in 1918 when the Germans recaptured the village. There were various methods for finding unmarked graves, for example, the colour of the grass might be different to the surrounding area, or sometimes evidence of a grave could be seen from burrowing rodents. Due to the fact that many of the identity discs were made of pressed fibre, most identity discs disintegrated, and therefore many of the graves found at Gavrelle were unidentified. About 80% were taken to Orchard Dump Cemetery and, to a lesser extent, to Point-du-Jour and Brown's Copse Cemeteries, the latter cemetery taking the many graves on Greenland Hill.

The missing, those who has no known grave, were to have their names on a Memorial to the Missing to be built in Arras. One of the hundreds of RND with no known grave was Able Seaman Simon Owen

Slowly the villagers came back to Gavrelle, building temporary huts, while constructing new houses. CAPRON FAMILY COLLECTION

The Mayor of Gavrelle, Louis Lequette, and the Mayor of the City of Westminster, J.F.C. Bennett, in 1930. Lequette with hat in hand, Bennett wearing top hat. (Henri Lequette)

James of the Anson Battalion who was killed at Gavrelle by shell fire whilst bringing up supplies to the Front Line. After the war his father found out the circumstances of his death, and was told that he had a proper burial. Unfortunately, in the battlefield clearance and the search for graves, no identified body was found. His mother could not come to terms with his death, refused to believe that he was dead, and for years afterwards kept his room ready for his return.

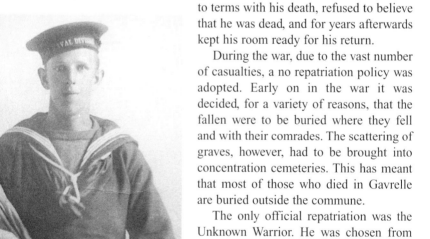

During the war, due to the vast number of casualties, a no repatriation policy was adopted. Early on in the war it was decided, for a variety of reasons, that the fallen were to be buried where they fell and with their comrades. The scattering of graves, however, had to be brought into concentration cemeteries. This has meant that most of those who died in Gavrelle are buried outside the commune.

The only official repatriation was the Unknown Warrior. He was chosen from four unknown graves taken from the Ypres, Arras, Somme and Aisne battlefields. He is called a warrior, instead

Able Seaman Simon Owen James, Anson Battalion, Royal Naval Division, 26 May 1917, No Known Grave, Bay I, Arras Memorial.

of a soldier, because he could be a soldier, an airman, or a sailor of the RND[3].

By the mid-1920s the village of the Gavrelle was nearly rebuilt, with the help of the City of Westminster, and also the family of sous-leiutenant René Gabias de Bagneris, the young cavalry officer killed in October 1914. This family was from Toulouse, and this is why St. Germain, the Patron Saint of Toulouse, is on the Gavrelle War Memorial. Both the Church and War Memorial were inaugurated in 1926.

The visible graves were exhumed from Gavrelle and concentrated into large cemeteries nearby, which in the early 1920s were officially declared closed, and perimeter walls built. With foundations being dug for new buildings and with the fields being ploughed again, even more graves were discovered. A few years after the war the body of Sub-Lieutenant Cleves was found in a field just north of Gavrelle; he was reburied at Cabaret Rouge Cemetery, north west of Arras. By 1926 this cemetery was becoming full, and Arras Road Cemetery was enlarged to take bodies being found during the late 1920s and early 1930s. Captain Arthur Kilby VC was found on the Loos battlefield, and reburied in Arras Road Cemetery, his name was taken off the Loos Memorial to the Missing. Most of the graves in Arras Road Cemetery are unknowns, and includes men of the Anson and Hood battalions. In the mid-1930s even this cemetery was becoming full, so Canadian No. 2 Cemetery on Vimy Ridge was enlarged and became the new open

Map 25: Main cemeteries around Gavrelle. Also shown is the location of the Arras Memorial to the Missing, to those who have no known grave.

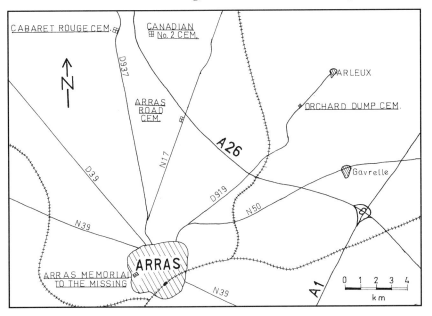

cemetery, not only for the Arras area, but even from the Somme area. In grave XIII.C.3 is an unknown company sergeant major of the RMLI found at Gavrelle. Also in this cemetery are the graves of two of the Red Baron's victims: Lieutenant Arthur Boultree (II.A.2) and Air Mechanic 2nd Class Frederick King, (II.A.1), who were shot down over Oppy on 17th March 1917 and buried by the Germans. Their names appear in the original 1926 edition of the Arras Memorial Register. During the early 1960s Canadian No.2 was almost full, and bodies still being found were taken to Terlincthun Cemetery near Boulogne. In the 1990s this policy changed, the discovery of new graves attracted much publicity and newly-found bodies are usually buried in CWGC cemeteries near where they were found.

In 1932 the Arras Memorial to the Missing was finally completed and inaugurated, to commemorate nearly 36,000 British, South Africans and New Zealanders who have no known grave[4]. Due to the Royal Naval Division being part of the 'Senior Service' the RND Naval Battalion's (RNVR) missing are listed on Bay One. Men from the Honourable Artillery Company, being one of the most senior regiments in the British Army, follow close by behind the hundreds of names from the RND Naval battalions.

The Arras Memorial Register states the area covered by the Memorial is from Loos to Berles-au-Bois, (10 kilometres south of Arras), however those killed in March 1918 show the geographical area to be further south than this, some even killed near to the site of the Thiepval Memorial on the Somme.

It was decided the memorial to the missing airman of the Great War should be sited at Arras, and just over 1000 names were put on a

Arras Memorial to the Missing, and Faubourg d'Amiens Cemetery.

column designed by William Reid Dick. On top of the column is a stone globe, set at the earth's axis on the eleventh hour of the eleventh month, 1918. This memorial lists all Allied airmen missing on the Western Front, even those who crashed in the English Channel. It was unveiled by Lord Trenchard, Marshal of the Royal Air Force, the father of the RAF on 31 July 1932. Although these two memorials are separate, the names were combined in the register of the Arras Missing. This register contains the most Victoria Cross recipients of any CWGC register, with a total of thirteen.

Soon after Germany invaded Poland on 1 September 1939, Britain and France declared war and a week later the BEF were once again sent to France. The War Graves Commission were still reburying newly found graves, and now had to prepare for graves of another war.

The BEF were sent to the Lille area, with General HQ at Arras. The 1/Royal Irish Fusiliers were stationed at Gavrelle. Once again the N50 was an important communication line between Arras and Douai, and the two villages of Gavrelle and Fresnes were used to billet British troops. The Royal Army Service Corps of the 1st Corps were at Fresnes, for servicing and fueling mechanised transport.

The 'phony war' (la drôle de guerre), was spent marching, exercising and fortifying the area. The Signal Corps in the area had the use of a mechanical trench digger for laying cables which could dig a trench two metres deep and two and a half metres long per minute, but for the average infantryman dugouts and trenches were dug by the age old method of pick and shovel. Near Fresnes a German helmet and a signal pistol from the previous war were dug up by troops preparing for another war with Germany. The RASC workshop at Fresnes reworked the metal into a football cup for winners of the football competition between British units in the Arras area[5]. The winter of 1939/40 was the severest for years, the ground froze and construction of cement pill-boxes was halted due to the cement-mix freezing.

On 10 May 1940 the Germans finally invaded, and swept through France, creating a corridor to the sea via Sedan, Amiens and Abbeville. The Luftwaffe, the aerial artillery of Blitzkreig, bombed the rail stations of Arras, Lens and Douai. Also targeted was the RAF aerodrome at Vitry-en-Artois. A counter attack was hastily planned to attack west of Arras, and cut the Panzer corridor in two. This action is well known, and documented, but the actions east of Arras are often overlooked.

150 and 13 brigades were sent to hold a line north of the River Scarpe, from Arras to Fresnes. The line from Fresnes to Douai was

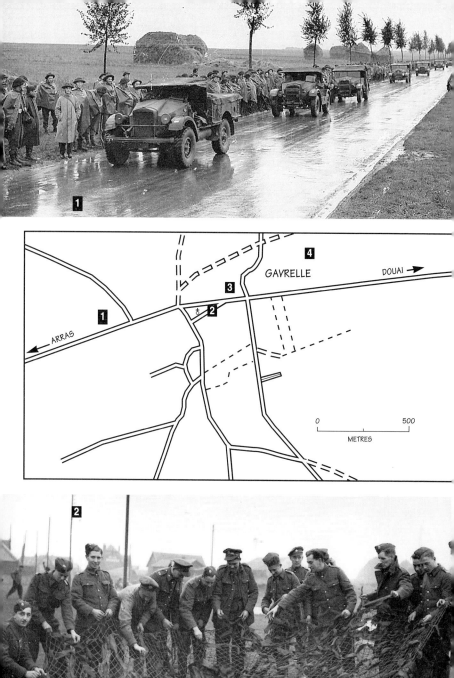

Location of BEF photographs taken in October and November 1939. The 1/Royal Irish Rifles were stationed at Gavrelle. There was an anti-aircraft Bofors gun near the site of the old windmill. Also shown are the RASC constructing a camouflage net on the village green. IWM

held by a French light mechanised division, a DLM (division légere mécanique). This line was not only to protect the flank of the counter attack, it would be the follow-up, when the attack west of Arras was successful in reaching Monchy-le-Preux. 150 and 13 brigades would cross the Scarpe and attack the retreating Germans along the Arras/Cambrai road. However, the attack, even though surprising the Germans and temporarily setting them back, was not really successful. The two brigades, instead of advancing south to support the breakthrough, had to fight a retreat action.

1/Welsh Guards were holding Arras, with the 4/Green Howards assisting them in the eastern suburbs of Arras, with the 4/East Yorks holding St Laurent-Blangy and Athies, and the 5/Green Howards holding the area north. Of 13 Brigade the 2/Wiltshires held Roeux and the 2/Royal Inniskilling Fusiliers were at Plouvain and Biache with the 2/Cameronians holding the area to the north, whilst C Coy of the Cameronians protected 13 Brigade HQ at Gavrelle[6]. The map below shows all the May 1940 graves east of Arras and north of the Scarpe, their locations show where the battalions were stationed, and also their lines of retreat. The battalions along the Scarpe retreated north, but the garrison of Arras, with a convoy of 40 vehicles, retreated east to Douai.

Map 26: Location of 1940 graves north-east of Arras. These graves show where the various battalions were stationed, and their lines of retreat. Partrols were sent out across the Scarpe and there are May 1940 graves in other communal cemeteries, but the River Scarpe is the southern limit of this guide. Note location of Vitry aerodrome and two RAF graves.

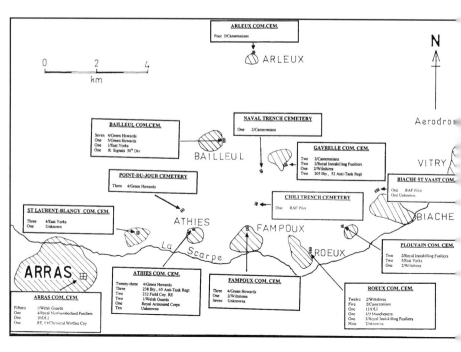

The N50 was under heavy shelling, so many of the side roads were used.

After the failure of the Arras counter attack, orders were given for Arras to be evacuated of British troops. On the night of 23/24 May Lieutenant Christopher Furness, 1/Welsh Guards, confronted Germans who had crossed the Scarpe. Furness and his Bren Carrier platoon attacked the Germans making it possible for the retreating convoy to continue to Douai. Furness was awarded the Victoria Cross. His body was never identified and he is commemorated on the Dunkirk Memorial to the Missing. His VC action took place about halfway between Arras and Gavrelle.

The location of Furness' action is often listed abstractly as 'near Arras'[7] or '3 miles from Arras'. In Athies Communal Cemetery Extension are two Welsh Guardsmen; Guardsman John Daly (who was the gunner of Furness' Bren Carrier), and Guardsman David Williams from Merthyr Tydfil (who was the gunner in one of the other two Bren Carriers in Furness' Platoon). Furness and Guardsman J. W. Berry (the driver of Furness' Bren Carrier) both have no known grave. There are ten unknown May 1940 graves in Athies Communal Cemetery Extension; is Furness VC buried under one of these unknown May 1940 headstones?

With the evacuation of the BEF at Dunkerque and through many other ports to the south, most of the BEF got back to Britain. Along with the evacuated British and French troops were 206 out of 540 War Graves staff and gardeners[8]. With the fall of France came another occupation. The Germans never captured Arras in the last war, but all of northern France was now under German occupation. The Gestapo took over the recently vacated War Graves Office in Arras[9].

At first there was only 'passive' resistance. All newspapers and broadcasts were controlled by the Germans, but an underground newspaper was printed for the Pas de Calais and Nord departments. It was called 'La Voix du Nord', the Voice of the North and its logo was the silhouettes of the smoky north; of the ports, factories, mines, workers' cottages, haystacks and windmills. The North is not the most picturesque part of France, but it was worth fighting for, to return to liberty and self-control.

In June 1941 Hitler disregarded the Nazi-Soviet pact, and invaded Russia. To the communists of the industrial north, Nazi Germany was

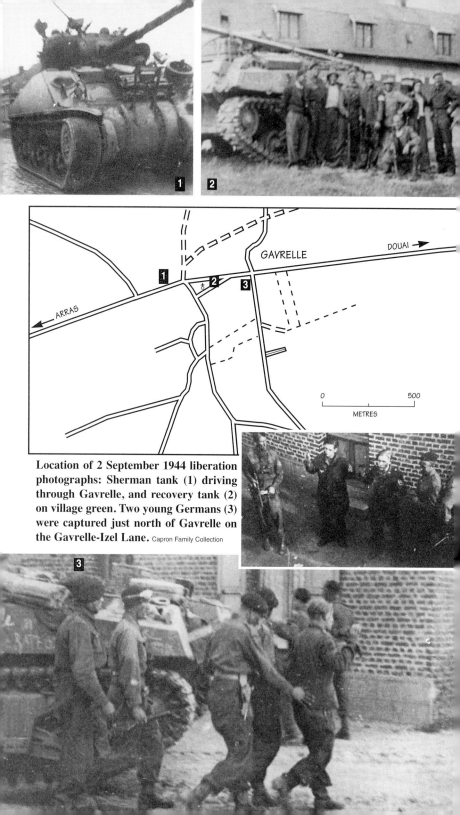

Location of 2 September 1944 liberation photographs: Sherman tank (1) driving through Gavrelle, and recovery tank (2) on village green. Two young Germans (3) were captured just north of Gavrelle on the Gavrelle-Izel Lane. Capron Family Collection

unquestionably now the enemy, and aggressive resistance started. The factories, mines, railway, canals, telephone lines and electricity supplies under German control became targets for sabotage. On 5 January 1943 the FTP (Francs Tireurs Partisans) sabotaged the electricity station at Gavrelle[10]. The Gestapo at Arras used the secluded dry moat area of the Arras Citadel to shoot 218 saboteurs and hostages from mid-1941 to mid-1944. This site is now a French national memorial.

The Germans were surprised by the Allied choice of Normandy for their invasion of Europe in June 1944, and reinforcements had to be sent to that area by rail. An intense Allied bombing of all rail junctions and marshalling yards had started months before the invasion, and this included the three towns of Arras, Lens and Douai. The Germans knew these vital lines would be attacked, and increased flak protection was introduced. Many Allied bombers were shot down and there are many isolated graves of aircrew in communal cemeteries in the Arras/Lens/Douai area. However, graves of aircrew do not necessarily denote a crashed aircraft. On a bombing raid on Lens on 11 August 1944, a Lancaster bomber (LL697) of 514 Squadron was hit in the nose by a bomb from another Lancaster and the bomb aimer fell out. Flight Officer Crampton RNZAF now lies in Loos Cemetery, just north of Lens. The rest of the crew (all RAF), made it back to Woodbridge airfield, but there was so much damage to the Lancaster that it was scrapped for spares[11].

Breaking out of Normandy, the Allies pushed eastwards. The Canadians and Polish divisions went up the coastal area and the British headed for Brussels via Amiens and Arras. Coincidentally, it was the

Welsh Guards in their spearheading tanks that liberated Arras. There was not much resistance, but more Welsh Guards graves were added to the area[12]. The tanks rushed along the N50 and passed through Gavrelle. The inhabitants, like all French villages and towns in the path of the liberators, put French flags in their windows, and cheered the liberators. Louis Lesart, who was wounded in the leg in May 1940, near Douai, had watched the Germans withdraw eastwards on the N50, and then came allied tanks, not seen for four long years. Cameras and film hidden from the Germans for the years of occupation were brought out to record this momentous occasion. Two young Germans were captured to the north of the village. A fenced-off cow field in Oppy was reinforced, and used as a 'cage' to hold temporarily all the Germans captured in the area[13].

The tanks of the Welsh Guards went to Vitry-en-Artois aerodrome where they were regrouped and reorganised; after a short rest, they rushed to liberate Brussels.

It was another eight months before the war ended, on 8 May 1945,

This photograph of three Bren Gun carriers in 1939 driving north out of Gavrelle, shows the old road to Oppy, bearing to the right, now a cul-de-sac, since the mid-1980s bypass was constructed. Part of the Café des Sports can be seen on the right. IWM 0164

which resulted in another street party. At least Gavrelle had not been destroyed this time, only slightly damaged. A plaque with nine names of Gavrellois killed in the war was put up on the Great War Memorial. One of the names is Pierre Carpentier, whose story is told elsewhere. (Chapter 10).

After the liberation of Strasbourg, Jacques Amar returned home to Gavrelle. He had been wounded in 1940 when fighting with the 3 Regiment Marche du Tchard and was evacuated to Britain. He landed at Normandy with the French forces, under General Leclerc, and went on to liberate Paris. Among his many decorations, Jacques Amar was awarded the Chevalier de la Legion d'Honneur, in October 1985, in a ceremony held by the Gavrelle War Memorial on the village green.

Post-war changes were subtle, but changed the landscape of the area considerably by the second half of the century. Peace brought progress, and technological advances. The aesthetically pleasing trees that lined main roads were cut down for road improvements, and not replaced, because they were causing deaths as the road traffic increased in volume and speed. The mechanisation of agriculture produced larger fields and also the disappearance of the iconic haystacks. These had been illustrated on trench maps as stars (*), left rotting on the battlefield, they were used as observation posts. A famous one known as 'the haystack' was just north of the N50 at Point-du-Jour.

The major changes to the area came in the mid-1960s when the A1 was constructed, to link Paris with the north, which ran through the south of the commune. In the early 1980s the A26 was constructed, the flyover bridge over the N50 was built on the old sight of 'Lonely House'. The A1 and A26 intersection lies at the boundaries of Gavrelle and Roeux, the connecting routes spread out to encompass the battlefield around Greenland Hill. In the early 1990s the TGV high-speed train line was constructed parallel to the A1, and yet again more of the battlefield was dug up, constructed upon and fenced off. During the early 1980s the inhabitants of Gavrelle were getting concerned about the high-speed traffic zooming through the centre of Gavrelle. Many fatal car accidents occurred, and the local paper published an article headed 'Gavrelle, une village morte'. The village primary school was next to the Mairie on the busy main road which caused much concern. A group was set up to protest to the local authorities and take direct action against those driving through the village. This finally led to a by-pass around Gavrelle, when the N50 was expanded into a dual carriageway. The by-pass constructed north of the village has unfortunately added considerably to the confusion in locating the

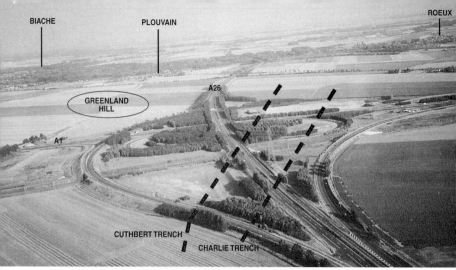

Aerial photograph, 1998 of the A1 and A26 Interchange south of Gavrelle, showing Greenland Hill, and Cuthbert and Charlie Trenches.

exact site of the old windmill. In the early 1990s the electricity station north of Gavrelle was enlarged, and more lines of pylons were constructed. In the mid-1990s a gas line was laid, which ran up from the Somme north, through Infantry Hill (east of Monchy-le-Preux), up to Gavrelle, passing under the N50 just west of Gavrelle and thence to the gas station west of Orchard Dump Cemetery on the D919.

The first part of this book has given the background history of the village in the 20th century. It is hoped an idea of the past landscape has been given to the visitor. The second part of the book focuses on what there is to see and visit in the hallowed acres of Gavrelle and the surrounding area.

1. City of Westminster Minutes of Proceeding of the Mayor, Alder and Councillors, March 1919.
2. Scott, P. *Captive Labour; the German Companies of the BEF, 1916-1920* in The Great War Journal, Vol.3, No.4, 1991, pp. 44-53.
3. *Courage Remembered*, (1989), by Ward and Gibson.
4. The Canadians have the names of their missing for all of France on the Memorial at Vimy Ridge. Sergeant David Jones, 14/Canadian Battalion, who was killed on the Trench raid led by Lt. McKean VC, has no known grave, his name is on the Vimy Ridge Memorial.
5. There is a photograph of the cup in the Photographic Department of the Imperial War Museum.
6. War Diaries of the 2/Cameronians (Scottish Rifles), May 1940, (PRO WO/9908).
7. *The Welsh Guards at War*, (1946) by Lionel Ellis.
8. *The Unending Vigil*, (1967), by Philip Longworth, (updated and reprinted in 1985), copies can be obtained from the CWGC at Maidenhead.
9. *The Shadow of Vimy Ridge*, (1967), by Kenneth Macksey.
10. *Quatre longues années d'occupation*, (1982) by André Coilliot.
11. *Bomber Command Losses of the Second World War*, 1944, (1997), by W.R.Chorley.
12. In Ecurie Communal Cemetary, (a few kilometres north of Arras), are seven graves of May 1940 and two Guardsmen, 2/Welsh Guards, both named Williams, both killed on 1 September 1944.
13. *Enfin libres septembre 1944*, (1994), published by La Voix du Nord

Chapter Seven

CAR TOURS

The car tour is based on ten cemeteries around the area. Most of the graves in and around Gavrelle were concentrated into existing cemeteries to the west. Information on the cemeteries has been put in a separate chapter, as they are also mentioned in the Walks chapter. This tour is a route guide to the cemeteries, pointing out relevant sites en route, whilst the cemeteries are put in the context of the surrounding landscape.

The tour starts at Naval Trench Cemetery.

Leave Gavrelle by the Oppy road (D33), drive under the N50, then turn right and stop at the field in front of you. Just to the south of where you can see two

Map 27: Route map of Car Tour of ten cemeteries.

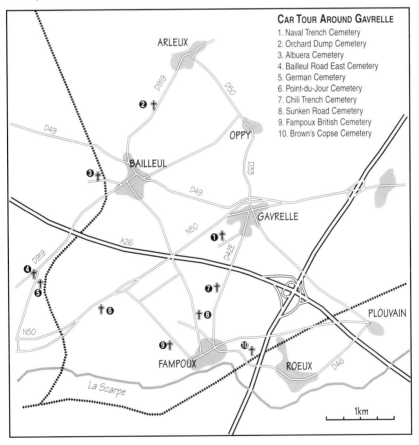

CAR TOUR AROUND GAVRELLE

1. Naval Trench Cemetery
2. Orchard Dump Cemetery
3. Albuera Cemetery
4. Bailleul Road East Cemetery
5. German Cemetery
6. Point-du-Jour Cemetery
7. Chili Trench Cemetery
8. Sunken Road Cemetery
9. Fampoux British Cemetery
10. Brown's Copse Cemetery

Aerial photograph of Gavrelle, 1998, looking north-west.

pylons in the field, is the site of the famous Gavrelle Windmill. Looking towards Oppy; opposite the electricity station, is the site of Cadorna Trench. Behind the electricity station were the trenches which Lieutenants Pollard and Haine, both

Map 28: Map of the area north of Gavrelle. The site of the Windmill, Cadorna Trench and the communication trench, Viscount Street, have been plotted.

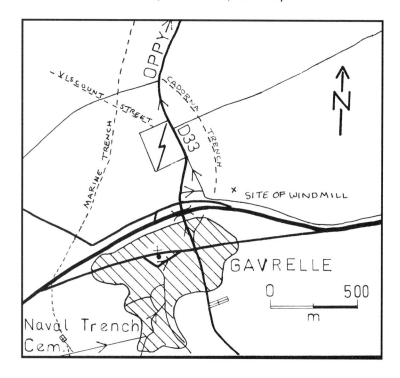

HAC, captured, and for these actions both were awarded the VC. Continue north to Oppy which, like Gavrelle, saw much fighting and destruction. In the village there is a monument to the Hull Pals of the 31st Division. If you climb the steps of this monument you can see into Oppy Wood, which is private property. Shell holes are still there and are quite visible when the undergrowth is not too thick.

Drive north through Oppy along the D50 to Arleux, which was captured by the Canadians on 28 April 1917. This Canadian victory is often overshadowed by that at the nearby Vimy Ridge. At the centre of the village, you come to a 'T' junction. (As a side trip, turn right and then left to the village communal cemetery, which contains five 1940 graves of the 2/Cameronians). Take the D919 to Bailleul, out of the village, and Orchard Dump Cemetery can soon be seen on your right.

Continue along the D919 into Bailleul. At the entrance to the village, on your left you will see

Map 29: Route from Oppy to Orchard Dump Cemetery.

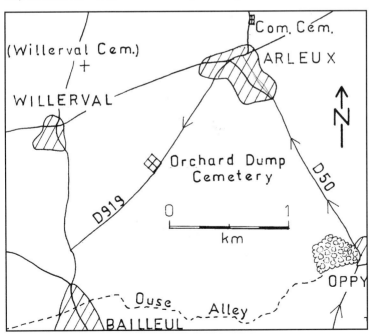

KINGSTON-UPON-HULL MEMORIAL

OPPY WOOD

D3

Oppy Wood in 1917.

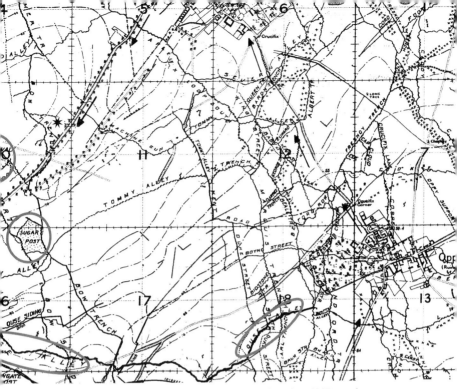

Map 30: Route from Oppy to Orchard Dump Cemetery, plotted on 1917 trench map. The star ✳ shows the site of the original cemetery, (B10 b 80.45), now most of Plot I. The strongpoints of Willerval South and Sugar Post along with Ouse Alley, have been highlighted.

a cow field with brick ruins; this was the Sugar Factory during the war. On 20 April 1917, while looking for cover during a bombardment, Second Lieutenant George Brown, 1/HAC, dived into a hole for cover. Unfortunately it was a well and he was drowned, a comparatively rare example of a member of the RND who was 'drowned in action'. George Brown has no known grave; his name is on the Arras

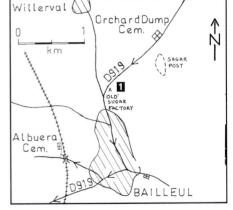

Map 31: Route from Orchard Dump Cemetery to Albuera Cemetery. Sugar post and the old sugar factory have been plotted.

Aerial photograph of German Cemetery and Bailleul Road East Cemetery. Looking south-west, with Arras in the background.

Memorial to the Missing. At the centre of the village, at a complicated (and dangerous) junction, turn right, and at the end of the village turn right again along a cobbled road and under a rail bridge to Albuera Cemetery.

Leave Bailleul on the D919, head south, and Bailleul Road East Cemetery will be seen in front of you and to the left and surrounded by trees, the St Laurent-Blangy German Cemetery. In the railway embankment, between the German Cemetery and Masion Blanche Wood, was the Divisional HQ for troops at Gavrelle. This dugout was called Haggis House and is mentioned in numerous Battalion War Diaries.

Continue south along the D919. On your right can be seen Roclincourt Aerodrome and Roclincourt Church steeple, rising from a dip in the land. This village contained a camp and was a rest area for the front line troops at Gavrelle. At the crossroads stands an isolated discotheque. Behind this is where the original frontline was before it was advanced on 9 April 1917. There

French Memorial Cross on German Pill Box marks the 9th April 1917 Front line.

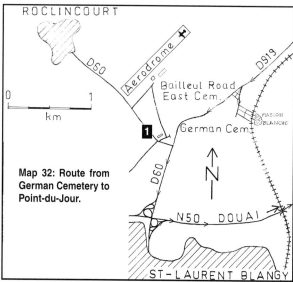

Map 32: Route from German Cemetery to Point-du-Jour.

is a German pillbox with a cross on it; this marks the German frontline. Roclincourt was used as major behind the lines base for the troops in the Oppy/Gavrelle area. Follow the signs to the N50 to DOUAI. Drive under the N50, then turn left to join the N50 east towards Gavrelle. Keep in the right (slow) lane as you will have to branch off to your right to reach Point-du-Jour Cemetery. Keep right, as this lane will soon be divided by a small concrete separation wall, drive past the cemetery and turn right into a parking area east of the cemetery. After visiting the cemetery, join the N50 again, taking care as in a short space you have to cross over from right to left to visit the 9th (Scottish) Division Memorial, which has a small section of original trench. It was from here that the RND attacked Gavrelle on 23 April 1917. (Those who are based in Arras can easily visit this monument and preserved trench on their way back to Arras, at the end of the tour.) Continue, by rejoining the N50, towards Gavrelle, slowing down when you go under the A26. This was the site of a house, known as Lonely House, which contained a small

Monument to the 9th (Scottish) Division with preserved trench at Point-du-Jour.

Gavrelle Demarcation Stone.

Map 33: Route from Pont-du-Jour Cemetery to Gavrelle, showing access to the 9th (Scottish) Division Memorial.

cemetery, later moved to Point-du-Jour. Just after the bridge, note the parking sign and park in the lay-by; here is the Gavrelle demarcation stone, which marks the limit of the final advance of the Germans in 1918. The steeple of Gavrelle church can be seen from here.

Continue along the N50, turn off to Gavrelle, and passing the memorial you will come to a mini-roundabout, turn back here towards the RND Memorial. Drive through the village, the caution signs on the road mark the village school, and the Mairie which has a plaque to the Queen's Westminster Rifles killed on 28 March 1918 on its wall. Turn right, then second right, en route to Fampoux. After crossing over the A26, you will see Chili Trench Cemetery on your right.

Continue south towards Fampoux, where the road dips out of view is the site of Hyderabad Redoubt, of which, sadly, there is no longer any trace. Just before you reach Fampoux, turn sharp left up a farm lane, keep right and continue to Sunken Road Cemetery. After visiting the cemetery, continue north. The road will become sunken; these steep sides were used for dugouts. Soon the area will flatten out into the Bailleul Valley. On the

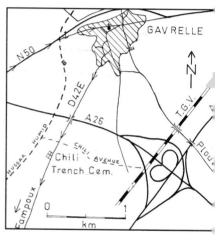

Map 34: Route from Gavrelle to Chili Trench Cemetery.

Aerial photograph of west Gavrelle looking south-east, showing the RND Anchor Memorial and Naval Trench Cemetery.

left of a (disjointed) crossroads of farm lanes was the original site of Northumberland Cemetery, but the sixty-nine graves (including Isaac Rosenberg's) were taken to Bailleul Road East Cemetery after the war. At this point there are two options. If the weather has been bad and your car could do without getting muddied, we recommend you turn around here and go to Fampoux British Cemetery via Fampoux. (See Map). If it is a sunny summer's day, continue up the lane until the lane branches off to the left. From here you can see where the A26 crosses over the N50. Where the bridge is was the site of Lonely House and about twenty-five graves from its garden were moved to Point-du-Jour Cemetery. Continue along this lane and take the second right towards Fampoux. Hidden behind a small copse is Fampoux British Cemetery.

After visiting this cemetery, continue along the lane to Fampoux, turn left and follow the signs through the village to Brown's Copse Cemetery.

Leave Brown's Copse Cemetery, turn left and go under the two train bridges, and over the A1 towards Roeux. On your right is Mount Pleasant Hill, (the western side contains two more CWGC cemeteries). In Roeux you will come to a crossroads where the village monument stands; this site was originally the village cemetery and

Aerial photograph of Chili Trench Cemetery, looking south-west.

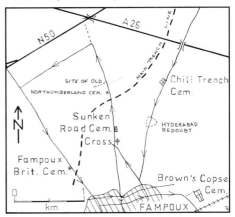

Map 35: Route from Chili Trench Cemetery to Brown's Copse Cemetery.

contained both British and German graves. Continue over the crossroads and shortly you will come to another crossroads, continue straight through, en route to Plouvain. On your left you will pass 'Lac Bleu', originally the site of Hansa Wood and Delbar Wood (with trenches). This area was turned into a large quarry after the war, then disused, and now turned into a water sports activity areas (the ever changing battlefield!). Continue over the A26 to the village of Plouvain where you will come to a crossroads. At this crossroads is a small monument to a 17 year old Resistance fighter shot on the road opposite the cemetery in 1944. Turn left, shortly you come to another crossroads (take care, another fast road with a blind bend). Continue straight across to Gavrelle. After crossing the railway line, you will notice a rise in the road. This is Greenland Hill, another little known slaughter ground of the Great War. Continue to Gavrelle where (if it is not a Sunday afternoon), the three cafes will be open, and Aubon Accueil and Relais de la Chaumiere provide meals for around 65F.

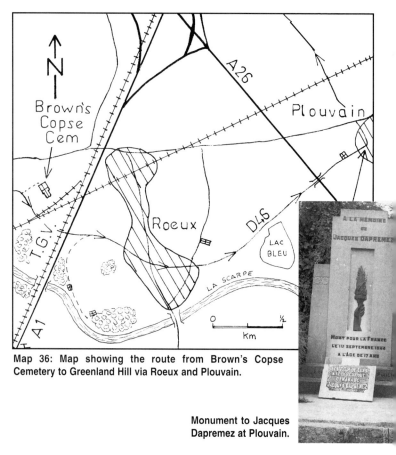

Map 36: Map showing the route from Brown's Copse Cemetery to Greenland Hill via Roeux and Plouvain.

Monument to Jacques Dapremez at Plouvain.

138

Chapter Eight

WALKS

WALK 1: AROUND GAVRELLE

This walk takes just over an hour. There is parking in the centre of the village, along the south road of the Church.

2 October 1914 French Memorial.

The walk starts at the 2 October 1914 memorial **(1)** to the French cavalrymen who confronted the Germans at the Windmill. This memorial is in the route impasse (now a cul-de-sac, created by the 1985 bypass), but was on the main road to Oppy. The memorial, built in 1967, is dedicated to twelve cavalrymen of the 23rd Dragoons, who were killed near here (on the Gavrelle-Izel Lane), by a German machine gun situated in the Windmill. This is also the site where a little Chapel stood, destroyed during the War, and never rebuilt.

Gavrelle War memorial.

Walking back to the centre of the village we come to the triangular green **(2)**, which contains the church and village memorial. At the apex of the green triangle is a 'Tree of Peace', planted on 8 May 1995, to

Map 37: Route plan of Walk around Gavrelle. The main points of interest are numbered 1-9. This walk takes about an hour and a half.

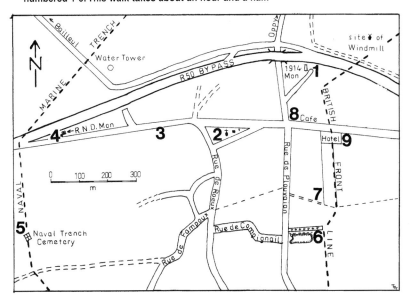

East end of Gavrelle Church, with 1940 shell damage, behind statue.

commemorate the 50th anniversary of the ending of the Second World War.

The village memorial contains the names of the village dead, which include two civilians, one being Victorine Capron, who was killed by a shell in the bombardment of Gavrelle, a few days before its capture on 23rd April 1917. Also on the monument is a plaque to the 34th French Infantry Division, which fought near Vimy Ridge in the Battles of Artois in 1915.

Also on the green is the village church. On the eastern wall is a statue to St Trerese erected in 1957; behind this statue, on the church wall, is a spray of fragment holes from a shell which burst nearby in May 1940.

The church was completely destroyed during the Great War and the new church was built in 1926, (not an exact replica, see illustrations). The old church was used as a hospital during the German occupation 1915-1917.

Due to present day security problems, the church is usually kept locked but if open when you visit you will find inside a plaque to those killed during the War (the same names as on the War Memorial). This is a frequent occurrence in France. The split between church and state was very strong in 1914, and this explains why almost every village has 'duplicated' war memorials and why the one outside rarely - if ever - has any overtly Christian symbolism about it. Another plaque

The old and new Gavrelle Church, 1916 and 1996.

The Hood Cross in the Church. This was commissioned and paid for by Arthur Asquith, the commanding officer of the Hood Battalion, when Gavrelle was captured by the RND. On the left looking at the memorial, is Captain Chris Page RN, who has recently written (1999) a military biography of Arthur Asquith.

records the connection and adoption of Gavrelle by the City of Westminster. Under the bell tower, on the north wall, is a wooden cross which has the names of the Hood Battalion lost at Gavrelle. This unusual memorial was commissioned and paid for by the commanding officer of the Hood Battalion, Arthur Asquith, the second son of the ex-prime minister. There are names on the Hood Cross, but this is a 1917 casualty list and present day research shows many more names should be on the cross.

Leaving the church and passing the community centre (where HMS Dragon and HMS Cambria stay during weekend ceremonial visits), head along the main road towards Arras. The Mairie was rebuilt in the same location. Stop at the Mairie, on the west side of the entrance is a plaque to the Queen's Westminster Rifles (3). The house next to the Mairie is owned by the Lesart family who, when they returned to their home after the war, found it all rubble with a large dugout, with thirty-two steps leading to it, below their cellar. In the early 1990s, when Louis Lesart was putting down a new floor in the front room, a signal flare gun was found.

Trench flare signal gun, found at Gavrelle.

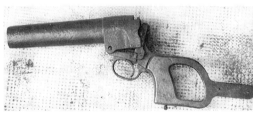

The Mairie, then and now. The one destroyed in the Great War (photograph taken c.1910), and its replacement built during the mid-1920s.

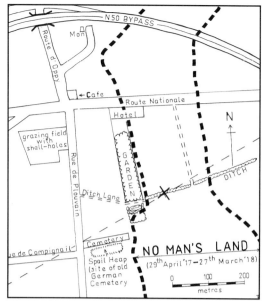

Map 38: The eastern area of Gavrelle showing Ditch Lane. The thin dotted line shows the path of the light railway; where it crossed the ditch (marked with a cross above), was the site of the drainpipe that Able Seaman Downe crawled through, 28 April 1917.

Carry on towards the bypass. Cars can drive down to the monument using the right separation lane. By the monument is a gap to turn back towards the village, but beware of cars exiting off the N50 towards Gavrelle at speed. For those walking, continue and the monument is on your right. On the horizon in the west, along the N50 to Arras, can be seen a group of trees and the 9th (Scottish) Division Memorial, looking like a small thimble on the horizon. This is the Point-du-Jour, and the RND started their attack on the village from here. On your left, looking south, is Naval Trench Cemetery, which marks the original German Front Line running north and south, through a line where the road to the village and new bypass meet.

Walk back to the Anchor memorial to the Royal Naval Division **(4)**, (see Chapter Ten for details on this memorial).

Walk back past the Mairie and turn right down the road to Roeux. This was the Yellow Line on which the RND halted to regroup and wait for the creeping barrage to move on. A few hundred yards along this road on your left was the site of the German monument made from shells. Continue along and take the road to Fampoux on your right, continue out of the village. On your right is a farm track to Naval Trench Cemetery **(5)**.

Walking back, take the Rue Compignail to come out by the village cemetery and spoil heap **(6)**. The large German cemetery was next to the village cemetery. During the war this cemetery, along with the village, was destroyed. After the war the scattered remains were removed to the mass burial plot

German occupation post card of the German Cemetery, (the village cemetery can be seen alongside in the background).

(*Kameradengräber*) at the German cemetery at St. Laurent Blangy. The site reverted to the village spoil heap.

In the communal cemetery are seven May 1940 graves. Also in this cemetery is a memorial to a priest who was deported to Germany and executed in 1943. This priest was brought up on a Gavrelle farm and had a parish in Abbeville, he was a reserve officer and was called up when war was declared. After the Fall of France, he went back to his parish in Abbeville where he made false documents for evading soldiers and airmen (see Chapter Ten for more details).

Continue up Rue de Plouvain, until you come to a lane on your right. This is Ditch Lane **(7)** where Commander Asquith and his party tried to reach the Mayor's house but due to intensive fire took another route. The lane is fenced off at the edge of the Mayor's garden (see map). About fifty metres further down the lane is where Asquith's party was forced back, leaving two dead. About thirty metres from this fence is where Able Seaman Downie crawled through the drainpipe, where the light railway crossed the ditch.

Turn back towards Rue de Plouvain, at the entrance is where one shell killed two of the Hood's company officers, Lieutenants Morrison and Tamplin. Continue north up the street to the crossroads and into the Cafe des Sports, Cafe-Tabac **(8)**. Inside the cafe is a copper plaque to the 31st Division, made by Veteran Joe Yarwood, who was a stretcher bearer and who spent his 21st birthday in a shell hole just to the west of Gavrelle in May 1917. The 31st Division took over from the RND at the end of April and took part in the costly 3 May 1917 attack.

The copper plaque, to the 31st Division made by veteran Joe Yarwood. The 31st was a Yorkshire and Lancashire Division, and a white and red rose was their Divisional badge. This memorial is in the Café des Sports.

Then and now photographs, (1915 and 1987), of Joe Yarwood, who was a stretcher bearer in the 31st Division.

The Mayor's House, rebuilt in 1922. It was a hotel, but is today used for conferences, as the outbuildings have been converted into Hotel Le Manoir.

Walk down the main road (towards Douai) and on your right you will come to Hotel Le Manoir. This was the Mayor's house **(9)** and is still owned by the descendants of the wartime mayor. Then, as now, horses are kept here. The house was rebuilt in 1922.

Continue out of the village (you are now in No Man's Land) and on your right a row of trees mark where the famous ditch was, and the site of the Sap of the German lines can be roughly worked out. The light railway ran diagonally across this field and during the 1990s a segment of the railway was ploughed up by a local farmer. Return to the village.

Gavrelle is fortunate to have three cafes in the centre of the village. Cafe de Sports has already been mentioned. Relais de la Chaumiere and Aubon Accueil provide meals for around 65F. All three cafes are closed on Sunday afternoon. However, Aubon Accueil is willing to open for coaches and provide sandwiches if prior notice is given.

Farmer Francis Dupayage with the section of the light railway ploughed up east of the Mayor's House in the 1990s. Note it is of all metal construction.

144

Then and now photographs of the eastern part of the main road through Gavrelle. Top; The 1/RIF marching through Gavrelle, October 1939. Below; the same scene today.

WALK 2: NORTH OF GAVRELLE

This walk starts near the site of the famous Gavrelle Windmill. The site of the Windmill has been plotted on some of the maps and aerial photographs, however, relating this information to the ground today is not so easy. The 1984 Bypass fortunately did not disturb the Windmill site but it did deflect the old Gavrelle to Izel-Les-Equerchin lane. This change has not been altered on French maps and has caused much confusion. The pylons in the fields help with an approximate location but care must be taken as many new pylons have been added recently and these are also not shown on modern maps. Not only do these pylons help locate the Windmill but the electric cables overhead make metal detectors virtually useless, and many of the secrets of the Windmill must still be buried there, below plough depth. After the War the Windmill was in ruins and this field was full of graves, mostly unknown RMLI who were reburied in Orchard Dump Cemetery. One of the RMLI killed and buried near the Windmill was Private Horace Bruckshaw, 2/RMLI, killed on 28 April 1917. His diaries were published in 1979 but, being killed during the fighting at Gavrelle, he never had the chance to write about his experiences here.

Across the road is the electricity station, which buzzes and crackles along with the songs of skylarks. In the August of 1992 the electricity station was extended southwards. One of the authors was on holiday at the time and every evening visited the site when the builders went home. One day a dugout or machine-gun post was uncovered, producing curved corrugated iron sheets and war debris. No graves were found (or reported found) and there is no information on what the workers took home with them as souvenirs, but lots of scattered personal equipment was found, webbing, water bottles, gas masks etc. While walking along a foundation ditch the author noticed something sticking out of the side and after much digging turned up a metal Vicker's machine gun ammunition box, which contained a belt of 250 bullets. Since the box was sealed, the canvas belt and bullets were in good condition considering it had been in the ground for nearly 80 years. This ammunition box was given to a museum in Arras. By plotting this site, this machine gun post seems to be on the junction between Brough Alley and Railway Trench. The foundation ditch being dug was for the south wall of the electricity station.

Walk back towards Gavrelle but, just before the bypass bridge, turn right, to the road to Bailleul. When the road bends, you will see the Gavrelle water tower. By standing on the north side of the water tower, looking north east towards Oppy, and lining the tower up with the corner of the electricity station, you can

Map 39: Route of Walk North of Gavrelle, (about 2 hours).

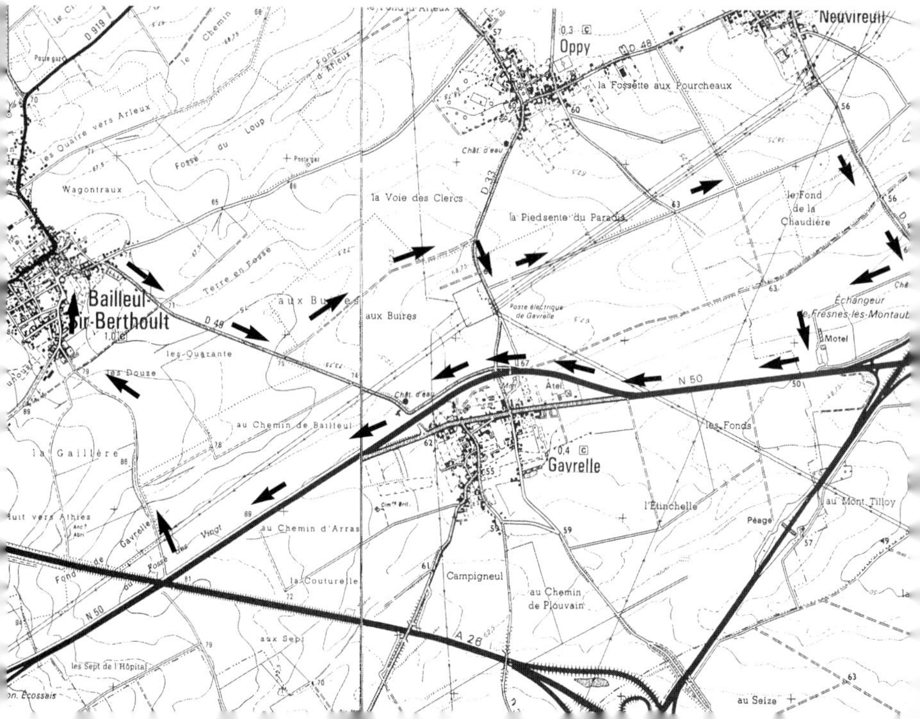

Concrete gun emplacement with 77mm German gun, near Vimy Ridge 1917. (NAC PA 2435)
Concrete gun emplacement north-west of Gavrelle, 1997.

roughly orientate the trenches where Lieutenants Pollard and Haine of 1/HAC bombed their way up the German trenches on 28 April 1917. Both were awarded the Victoria Cross for these actions.

Cross over the road to the agricultural lane going south west, running parallel to the N50.

Walking along this lane, on your right would have been the German communication trench

Vickers machine gun ammunition box, with 250 bullets, dug up in August 1992 when the Gavrelle Electricity Station was enlarged. Found in the foundation trench for the south perimeter fence.

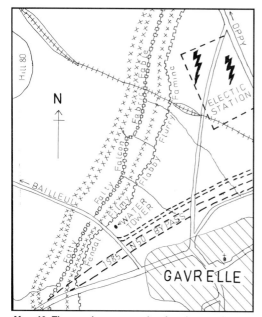

Map 40: Then and now map showing the positions of the VC trenches. By lining up the Gavrelle water tower and the north-west edge of the electricity station, the rough location of the trenches which Lieutenants Pollard and Haine of the HAC bombed their way along the German Trenches on 29 April 1917 may be established. Both were awarded the Victoria Cross.

called Gavreller Weg. When Gavrelle was captured this German trench was used as the main communication trench to north Gavrelle and renamed Thames Alley. Where the A26 crosses over the N50 is the site of the Lonely House and the 1918 demarcation stone. Just north of this was the site of the strong point known as Ditch Post.

At the A26 flyover bridge you have a choice of routes, depending on the mud conditions and your footwear. Those wishing the easy route can take the lane to Bailleul. The more adventurous can walk along the base of the embankment. There is no path as such, but it is possible to walk on the grass strip between the A26 fence and the field. Soon you will come to another lane, turn right towards Bailleul. On the right of the lane you will see a few trees and some undergrowth. In this undergrowth is a German concrete gun shelter.

If you visit in the winter you will undoubtedly plough through much mud. However, if you visit in the summer there will be so much undergrowth that access will be restricted. So, whenever you visit, this site will not be easy to get to but the access problem has contributed to its preservation, and it is the only covered gun pit in the area. This gun emplacement seems a typical construction for a 77mm gun, concrete covered with metal front covers. The direction of fire enables it to cover an arc from the Labyrinth to Vimy Ridge.

Also in this area (B.27), crashed one of Manfred von Richtofen's victims, on 16 April 1917. The BE2e crashed just inside the British lines. The pilot, Lieutenant Alphonso Pascoe, was wounded and recovered, but the observer, Second Lieutenant Frederick Andrews, was taken to Le Touquet hospital on the coast and died of wounds on 29 April 1917; he is buried in Etaples Military Cemetery.

Pascoe and Andrews were the 45th victims of the Red Baron, and they are unique in the fact that this claim was thought to have been another BE2e crewed by Lieutenants W. Green and C.E. Wilson. Green and Wilson were operating in the St. Quentin area and have been eliminated as the Red Baron's 45th victims because of the flying distance from St. Quentin and Gavrelle. Added to all this, Richtofen, in his letters and reports, spelt Gavrelle with a 'C' rather than a 'G'. Even in the 1990s these mistakes are still perpetuated in books and on the Internet. The crew were undoubtedly Pascoe and Andrews, who crashed near here, between Bailleul and Gavrelle. There is no village in the north of France called Cavrelle. There are many examples of the mis-spelling of Gavrelle in books and on maps, which has helped to hide so much of the history of Gavrelle. In the communal cemetery in Douai, the cemetery register reads:-

ADENEY, 2nd Lt., Robert Edward. 3rd Bn. The Queen's and 48th Sqdn. Royal Flying Corps. Died of wounds received in air combat at Gavielle [sic], 11 April 1917. Age 19. Son of William Henry and Mary Adeney, of 16 Sackville St., Piccadilly, London. (Grave D.8).

Second Lieutenant Adeney was flying a new Bristol Fighter and his rear gunner, Second Lieutenant L.G. Lovell, also died but has no known grave. He was presumably buried on the battlefield, while Adeney was taken to the German hospital at Douai.

Also shot down near Gavrelle on 11 April 1917 were Lieutenants G.T. Morris and J.M. Souter, flying in an RE8. In Trevor Henshaw's book, *The Sky Their Battlefield*, working from war diaries, Henshaw gives the map reference for the crash site as B.28 a.8.5. The CWGC Burial Returns state that the graves of these two airmen were removed from B27 b.3.1. Both of these map references of the crash and burial site can be seen on the grid map below. Lieutenants Morris and Souter are now buried side by side in Orchard Dump Cemetery, 3 kilometres to the north.

The above two examples of RFC planes being shot down on the same day, and within sight of each other, shows how intense 'Bloody April' was over the skies of Gavrelle. However, the battle was not all one sided. German planes also crashed in this area, including a decorated German ace.

Sergeant Sabastian Festner from Bavaria was originally an air mechanic but

Map 41: The crash site of the Red Baron's 45th Victim. Illustrated is pilot Alphonso Pascoe, RFC. On 16 April 1917, when flying a BE2E, he was shot down and crashed at grid reference B27 d or c, Pascoe survived the war, but his observer, died of wounds.

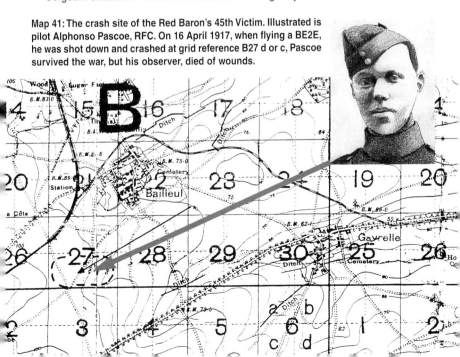

learnt to fly and by November 1916 was a pilot in Jasta 11, near Douai, better known as the Red Baron's Flying Circus. In early February he shot down his first plane; his fourth victim on 5 April was piloted by Captain William L. Robinson, who had been awarded the VC for shooting down a Schutte-Lanz Airship over London on 2 September 1916. Festner went on to shoot down a total of 12 aircraft but he too became a victim of Bloody April.

On 25 April 1917, while the RND were consolidating Gavrelle from counter attacks, several planes were in the sky above, one of them being Festner's Albatross DIII. Between Bailleul and Gavrelle Festner crashed and was killed. Like Richtofen a year later, there is controversy as to how Festner was killed, some sources say his propeller broke, some say he was shot down by the RFC, some that he was hit by ground fire. How he died may never be known but he did crash in this area, another pilot and aircraft to come to grief whilst flying over Gavrelle. (Some sources state he crashed between Oppy and Gavrelle).

Continue along the lane towards Bailleul-sir-Berthoult. This large village is sited halfway along the Arras-Lens railway line and before the war had a sugar factory, destroyed during the war, which converted the sugar beet crops of the surrounding area. It was never rebuilt. Bailleul had a population of just under 1000 before the war and now has just over 1000 inhabitants. As you enter the village, keep bearing right until you exit the village by the D49 towards Gavrelle. On the outskirts of the village, on your right, is Bailleul Communal Cemetery. In this cemetery are nine May 1940 graves. These are a mixture from the 5th and 50th Divisions, showing the retreat from the Scarpe and Arras, after the failure of the Arras counter attack of 21 May 1940. One of the graves is Second Lieutenant Alexander Christopher King of 4/Green Howards, killed on 24 May 1940, aged 24. He was a solicitor before the war.

Continue along the D49 to Gavrelle, but take the second lane on your left towards the Gavrelle electricity station. On your left is 'Hill 80' but modern agriculture has smoothed out this strategic little rise that housed the Bailleul East Post strongpoint. This area was covered in graves, most, but not all, of the graves north of Gavrelle were reburied in Orchard Dump Cemetery. At B24 a.2.9, Private J. Luke, 1/HAC, (killed on 23rd May 1917), was reburied after the war in Point-du-Jour Cemetery (II.E.23). When nearly opposite the electricity station, about where overhead cables cross the lane, was where the communication trench Viscount Street ran. Just north of here was the battalion HQ and an aid post for the area south of Oppy Wood, which contained a small cemetery of over thirty-four graves at B24 b.2.5. These graves, (mainly unknown of the RND and 31st Division), were concentrated into Orchard Dump Cemetery. One of these graves was an unknown British officer.

Where the lane joins the Oppy-Gavrelle road B24 b. 2.9. was another cluster of graves. Out of the twelve graves found, only two could be identified; Private Napier RMLI (identified by his name on his spoon and cigarette case), and Private Stephens RMLI (identified by name on disc and watch). The rest are only partially identified as RMLI and two only as being 'British' by their khaki uniforms. These twelve graves are now in Orchard Dump Cemetery, plot VII.

At the Gavrelle-Oppy road, turn south towards Gavrelle, when alongside the entrance to the electricity station, in the field opposite, running in an arc, would have been Cadorna Trench, which was successfully captured on 28 June 1917.

At this point there is a choice of either finishing the walk by walking back to Gavrelle or continue along the lane opposite to circle around the Motel and back to the Windmill site. This area takes the view of the German side. While there is not much to see today, this walk will show Gavrelle from the east, the many dips in the ground for shelter, and the excellent field of fire between Fresnes and Gavrelle, which made it so difficult for the British to advance out from the protection of the ruins of Gavrelle. How many German graves were in this area we do not know. Thousands were reported killed during the many counter attacks on Gavrelle, as well as the capture on 28 March 1918. About halfway between Gavrelle and Fresnes, just north of this lane, (C20 c.5.4), was a British grave but it could not be identified, only partially identified by his 'Hood' shoulder title. His grave is now in Orchard Dump Cemetery (II.E.16). This area is about one grid square (1000 yards) behind the German Front Line, and this RND sailor could have died at a German aid post and been buried nearby.

WALK 3: SOUTH OF GAVRELLE

This walk is a circular tour south of Gavrelle and can be joined at any point of the route. For the sake of convenience the tour starts at Biache-Saint-Vaast. The walk is about four hours, excluding stops and time spent in cemeteries.

Biache has a population of just under 2000, and with its communication lines of the Paris-Lille railway and the canalised River Scarpe, has a long history of

Map 42: Route of Walk South of Gavrelle, (about 4/5 hours).

heavy industry, including an important cement factory and sheet metal plant supplying the automobile industry. In 1976 archaeologists found a prehistoric skull here which is now in Paris at the Musée de l'Homme.

The walk starts on the bridge over the River Scarpe. Walking north, on your right is the site of the old cement factory. This factory produced cement for the pillboxes and blockhouses of the area. Its tall conspicuous chimneys are marked on trench maps. Destroyed towards the end of the Great War, the factory was used once again by the Germans to help build the Atlantic Wall during the Second World War. The cement factory finally closed in the late 1980s and its three 80 metres high chimneys were demolished. Just past the old entrance to the factory is a monument to workers of the factory who were executed for sabotaging the factory in 1941.

German monument at Fresnes.

This main road has an unusually high number of cafes (to cater for the large number of workers at the factories). There is also a supermarket (closed on Mondays), which can be used to stock up with food and drink for the walk. Near the supermarket, turn west down Rue Clemenceau. At the end of this road is a wall with a small plaque which states that one of the French Resistance leaders, Charles Delestraint, lived in this house. Delestraint was born in Biache in 1879 and was executed in Dachau in 1945. Walking north, take the first right and walk down Rue Edouard Herriott, then turn left at the end of this road, to join the main road again.

On your left will be a small park, Square Massenet. Trench maps show this site was originally a cemetery and could have been the site of German graves. Continue north, across the rail track and on the outskirts of Biache is the communal cemetery. Besides French war graves and monuments, there are three

Map 44: Trench map of the Fresnes area. The route of the walk to Railway Copse has been marked on the trench map.

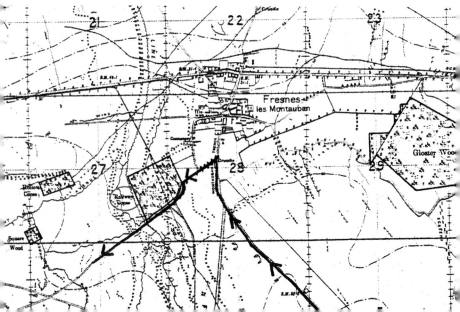

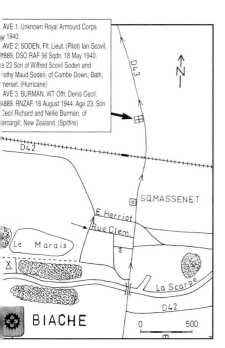

Map 43: Route through Biache.

CWGC headstones, one an unknown soldier of 1939-1945 and the other two are pilots.

Flight Lieutenant Soden RAF, flying a Hurricane of 56 Squadron, was shot down by a Me 110 on 18 May 1940. The aerodrome of Vitry-en-Artois was attacked by the Luftwaffe on 17 May 1940 and Soden shot down a Heinkel 111 bomber. While on dawn patrol the next morning he shot down a Dornier bomber which crashed six kilometres to the south. The next raid on the aerodrome the bombers had a fighter escort, and Soden was shot down while taking off and crashed just outside the perimeter of the aerodrome.

Warrant Officer Burman RNZAF was flying a Spitfire of 74 Squadron and was shot down by ground fire on 16 August 1944. Burman was born in England but his parents emigrated to New Zealand when he was five years old. Burman enlisted in the RNZAF, served in many squadrons and saw action in the Western Desert, damaging two enemy aircraft and shooting down one, before he was also shot down in the desert. Burman joined 74 Squadron in June 1944 and flew a Spitfire escorting bombers and ground strafing. On the day he was shot down he was en route for Cambrai. The report in the New Zealand Defence Force Archives says he was shot down by machine gun fire and baled out near Doueix [sic], France. In the History of the 74 Squadron, Bob Cossey states that Burman, after being hit, gained height in order to bale out safely and landed in the village of Roeux but was shot on the spot by German troops.

Taking into account the westerly prevailing wind of the area, Burman may have been shot down over Roeux, but his parachute probably drifted towards Biache, and this could be the reason why Burman is buried in Biache Cemetery and not Roeux Cemetery.

After leaving the cemetery, continue walking north to Fresnes-les-Montauban. On your right you will see a large wood (known as Gloster Wood) and a smaller wood on your left, known as Railway Copse during the war. These woods were used to assemble German troops for the numerous attacks on Gavrelle and were subsequently heavily shelled by artillery.

As you enter Fresnes, a lane branches off to the left. The trench map has a 'crucifix' marked on it. This calvary was destroyed during the Great War and never rebuilt, however, the two steps up to the calvary are still there to mark the site.

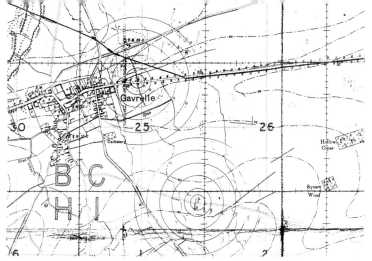

Map 45: Artillery Ranging Clock Circles on trench map of Gavrelle. These are centred on the two main German routes to Gavrelle, the roads from Fresnes and the road from Biache.

Take the turning left just after the steps and walk towards Railway Copse. After about 60 metres on your left you will come to a farm entrance flanked by sheds, near here is the German monument with artillery damage. If this monument is on its original site, a German cemetery could have existed between monument and the calvary, now occupied by cow sheds. Only further research can confirm this speculation.

Continue towards Railway Copse. This is private property but by looking over the wire the uneven ground caused by shell holes can be seen. The trench maps show a railway junction in the wood, hence its name.

The construction of the A1 deflected the original path of this lane, and also swallowed up the sites of Hollow Copse and Square Wood of the Great War battlefield.

Walk along this lane, which runs along the autoroute, until you come to the Gavrelle-Plouvain road. On your left is Greenland Hill, which may not look like a hill today but in 1917, when heavily fortified, was a formidable feature of the landscape. Turn north towards Gavrelle, over the A1 and over the TGV.

Near this road, at H6 c.5.4, was the grave of an unknown officer of the Essex Regiment. After the war his remains were taken to Brown's Copse Cemetery (Plot VII, Row A).

Also lost along with Hollow Copse and Square Wood, (due to the construction of the autoroute), was the old road to Biache. This road, along with the Gavrelle-Fresnes road, were the main German reinforcement routes to Gavrelle.

The trench map shows the concentric rings used by the RFC while directing artillery. These are centred on the two communication lines and were probably used either to stop reinforcements moving up, or even breaking up a counter attack by the Germans. These concentric rings were known as 'Clock Circles'. The RFC would observe where a preliminary shell fell and then signal back to the artillery. These circles were given alphabetical classification and, using a clock system, a point within the circles could be located. For example, in the top

154

circle, if a shell aimed at the road landed by the Windmill, that would be circle 'D' at 11 o'clock. This information was signalled to the artillery and the appropriate adjustments made to the guns.

Even though the lane to the east is lost, the connecting road to the west is still there today, so the site can be found. There are allotments on your left, this is the site of the strongpoint called Towy Post. The road to Gavrelle now dips into a hollow and is the 'sunken lane' where Commander Sterndale Bennett and his Drake Battalion took shelter on 23 April 1917. You can see how strong a defensive position this was, but also how vulnerable it would be to advance to the east from here.

Continue into Gavrelle. Meals and drinks can be obtained in Gavrelle, except on Sunday afternoon.

Leave Gavrelle by the Fampoux road, going south. After crossing the autoroute, Chili Trench Cemetery can be seen on your right. Ahead of you, where the road dips towards Fampoux, was the site of Hyderabad Redoubt. After descending the bridge over the autoroute, on your right, you should notice a very slight valley, this is Bailleul Valley. On your left, in line with the valley, ran the communication trench called Chili Avenue, which gave its name to the cemetery.

Near Chili Trench Cemetery was a grave (I1 d.9.9)and the only form of identification was a 'star' (pip) on a khaki epaulet. The remains are today under a headstone which reads "Unknown 2nd Lieut. of the Great War", in Brown's Copse Cemetery (V.C.7).

After visiting Chili Trench Cemetery, continue along the D42E to Fampoux, but after about 100m take the turning on your right, along an agricultural lane.

Aerial photograph, 1998, of Chili Trench Cemetery looking west, also showing the site of the old Northumberland Cemetery, where the artist and poet Isaac Rosenberg was originally buried. The centre of the photograph is the area where the Canadian Lieutenant George McKean's actions on a trench raid, the night of 27/28 April, resulted in the award of the Victoria Cross.

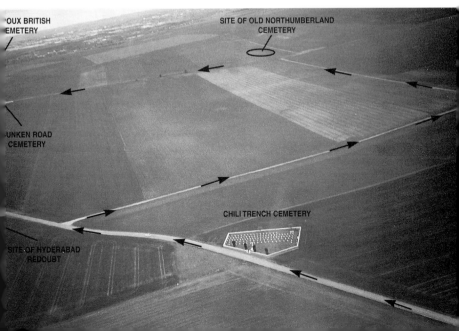

This is the area where both Cassiday and McKean's trench actions gained them the VC. By using this lane, the cemetery site, and the then and now map, it should be possible to locate roughly Humid and Hussar trenches which are now sadly completely smothered under modern agricultural use. The fields here rotate from sugar beet, hay and peas. These fields are private property. Due to the extensive fighting here, battlefield debris can sometimes be seen at the edges of the fields alongside the lane. Walk down the lane and, where it turns left, you are walking along Bailleul Valley where the Germans advanced in late March 1918.

At the end of the lane you will come to a sunken road. This lane was known as Northumberland Lane and Northumberland Cemetery was near here (H11.a.6.5), alongside the lane. This cemetery had over 70 graves, including the artist and poet Isaac Rosenberg, but this cemetery was concentrated into Bailleul Road East Cemetery, 3½ km to the north west.

As a side trip you can continue north to the site of Lonely House, which also contained graves, but these were concentrated into Point-du-Jour Cemetery.

Continue south down Northumberland Lane and soon the banks either side become many metres high; this sunken stretch of the lane was honeycombed with dugouts, aid posts and HQ. Look carefully at these sides, as now and again a dugout collapses, making a sunken hole. After a short walk, on your left you will see Sunken Road Cemetery. This cemetery, with its view of the battlefield, makes an excellent stop for a rest and consumption of packed vitals, whilst the base of the Cross of Sacrifice provides a seat to view the eastern battlefield including, in front of you, the site of Hyderabad Redoubt.

After visiting the cemetery, continue south towards Fampoux. After a few minutes you will come to the Seaforth Highland celtic cross, erected to the memory of the seven battalions of the Regiment which fought in this area. The cross marks the starting point of the costly attack on Roeux of 2/Seaforth Highlanders on 11 April 1917.

At the crossroads near the celtic cross, take the second right lane to Fampoux. On the outskirts of Fampoux you will come to the village cemetery. There are ten CWGC May 1940 graves here but only four are identified, of these three are from 4/Green Howards and one from 2/Wiltshires. The other six are unknown. Two French Resistance fighters were apprehended in this cemetery on 9 June 1944 and deported to Germany.

Continue south along Rue du Four and turning left at a cafe on to Rue Paul Verlaine. The poet Paul Verlaine (1844-1896) spent his summer school holidays in Fampoux, where his aunt lived. On this road is the Brewery Bécu, founded in 1862 and destroyed, along with the rest of the village, during the Great War.

Fampoux in 1919, Rue d'Enfev.

When the brewery was rebuilt the ancient symbol for prosperity and wellbeing was incorporated into the brickwork. However, the Nazis adopted the (clockwise) swastika symbols to represent the National Socialist Party. There are two swastika symbols on the building, clockwise and counter-clockwise. This portrays the yin and yan balance of these two ancient symbols. The shop on the main road through Fampoux (D42) sells L'Atrébate beer. The beer takes its name from an ancient tribe that lived in the area.

Near the end of Rue Paul Verlaine, in the ruins of a house on your right (H17 d.65.65), was the site of the original grave of Trooper Sykes, Household Battalion, killed on 11 April 1917. He was reburied in Point-du-Jour Cemetery (III.J.4). Trooper Sykes was identified by "papers in pocket". At the end of this road you will come to Place Public. Take the road south (Rue des Etanges) to the River Scarpe. Following the Scarpe, go under the railway bridge. At this bridge, on 8 July 1846, the train to Paris was derailed and coaches rolled down the embankment, some ending up in the small lake. This was one of France's first major rail accident.

Continue along this road which bends to the left, go under two sets of rail bridges and on your right you will see Brown's Copse Cemetery.

After visiting this cemetery, go back under the railway bridges, and over the TGV and A1 towards Roeux. On your right you will see Mount Pleasant Hill. During the Great War a rail line was extended to the woods. A large rail gun fired at Arras and as far away as Doullens. This area is also riddled with tunnels used by both sides during the war. They contain graffiti on its walls, even in Welsh, when the Welsh Guards were here in early 1918.

In Roeux you will come to a crossroads. The triangular site where the village monument now stands used to be the village cemetery. British graves were taken from here to Point-du-Jour cemetery after the war. Continue across and

Aerial photograph, 1998, showing the route through Fampoux.

Montage of images drawn on the walls of the tunnels under Rouex. These tunnels are no longer open to the public, but there is always hope that things will change in the future. The tunnels are named after the trenches above, Ceylon, Corona, Mount Pleasant. These are indicated on the Trench map, Map 18, page 87.

shortly you will come to another crossroads. Turn left and walk to the village cemetery, which contains thirty-three CWGC May 1940 graves. There is also a small monument to the village civilians killed in the May 1940 bombardment. On the cemetery shelter there is a small French Resistance plaque. Walking back to the crossroads, turn left out of Roeux, on the road to Plouvain.

Leaving Roeux on the D46, you will soon come to the water sports area of Lac Bleu. There was a small quarry and woods in this area but after the war the quarry was greatly expanded for its limestone, mainly to provide the material for making cement. There is a cafe and brasserie here, and if open is worth a visit as the walls are lined with photographs of the history of the quarry. When the quarry closed down, it was turned into a water sports facility. During August this area is swarming with visitors. Bathing is not allowed as there are no life guards, but this does not stop the local youths. One of the authors has found Lac Bleu convenient to bath his feet after a long walk on a hot summer's day.

Rejoin the D46, continuing east, over the A26, and you will see Plouvain in front of you and on your left Plouvain Communal Cemetery. When the Germans were retreating out of Arras, on 1 September 1944, a column of German vehicles came along this road and were attacked by the French Resistance. Jacques Dapremez, only 17 years old, was shot and wounded. He crawled into the cemetery and was bayoneted to death. A plaque on the cemetery floor marks the spot where he died. Also in this cemetery are six CWGC May 1940 graves, of which one is unknown. Four graves are by the entrance and two by the west wall.

Leave the cemetery, turning left towards Plouvain. On the right hand side of the crossroads is a small monument to Jacques Dapremez. Continue towards Plouvain church, turn right at the cafe towards the Scarpe; after crossing a stream and passing fishing ponds, in a wooded area you will come to a lane crossroads. Take the left turning towards Biache, passing the camping site.

This last route is only suitable for walking or cycling, those doing this tour by car should take the D42 to Biache.

Chapter Nine

THE CEMETERIES

INTRODUCTION

This chapter gives information on the ten cemeteries mentioned in the Car Tour and the Walks chapters. Nine are Commonwealth War Graves Commission (CWGC) cemeteries, but one German cemetery is included and some of the cultural differences between national cemeteries are explained.

Every CWGC is a potential research library, not only has it a cemetery register on the site (if not stolen), but the headstones themselves are like documents, instead of being on a shelf they are set in rows. The cemetery registers contain, in alphabetical order, identified graves, or Special Memorials (SM). SM are headstones with no bodies underneath and are either to known graves destroyed by artillery or else are "Known to be buried in this cemetery", where records show the person was buried in the cemetery but the precise grave is not known.

Apart from the total number and nationality, the unknowns are not mentioned in the cemetery registers, but there is much information to be gleaned from reading the headstones. The unknown can be divided into two groups, the unknown and the partially unknown. With the unknown very little was found, only khaki uniform, buttons or boots, to help distinguish the body from that of an unknown German soldier. The partially unknown are identified mostly by regiment or unit, (from metal shoulder titles), or by rank, and sometimes the date of death is known. These scraps of information are inscribed on the headstones.

It is a popular misconception that most of those missing in the Great War were pulverised by artillery; this is a myth, as most were buried, but on many occasions it was their grave markers, rather than the graves themselves, which were destroyed by artillery. During the Great War the majority of identity discs were made of pressed fibre and these soon rotted in moist soil. When the Germans attacked in March 1918 they were stopped after a few kilometres, but many cemeteries were now in the Front Line and grave markers were destroyed in the fighting. After the war, when graves were exhumed, the identity discs had rotted away and in some cases all the identity that remained was the metal shoulder title. Most graves did not have even this and now are under a headstone with the inscription "An Unknown Soldier of the Great War . . . . . Known unto God".

Some of the concentration graves have their original place of burial stated. Most of this information comes from CWGC 'burial returns'. These documents do not contain much detail, but do shown where the body was found, by trench map grid reference, and what was found to identify, or partially identify, the body. These documents are difficult to access from the CWGC and we hope we have used them to create greater interest in, and understanding of, the CWGC cemeteries.

1. NAVAL TRENCH CEMETERY

This small battlefield cemetery contains sixty graves, (including one Second World War grave). This cemetery derives its name from the German defensive trench west of Gavrelle which was renamed Naval Trench when captured by the RND. A communication trench, Towy Alley was dug south of the Arras-Gavrelle road, and this cemetery was near the junction of these important trenches, as was a battalion HQ dugout, and an aid post.

The fifty-nine Great War graves in this cemetery are from three Divisions: the 31st, 47th and the RND. Private Titford of the 11/East Yorks is the only member of the 31st Division in the cemetery. He was killed on 14 May 1917, there was only one other of this battalion killed on this day, Private George Higginbottom, and he has no known grave; his name is on the Arras Memorial to the Missing.

The RND have the most graves; totalling about half the graves in this cemetery. The Anson Battalion have nineteen graves, nearly one-third of the total. The day on which most Ansons were killed was 7 September 1917. Consulting the Anson War Diaries for this date shows a raid took place on 'the Sap'. The War Diary states that this raid was a success, with only one casualty, last seen in No Man's Land, and now missing, presumed dead. So the four Ansons killed on this date were not on the raid. The War Diary goes on to state that the enemy retaliated with a bombardment of the strongpoints and communication trenches, particularly shelling Towy Alley.

There are no RND graves for 23 April 1917, the day the RND captured this area, but there are two Hawke Battalion sailors who were killed on 24 April. The Hawke Battalion was in reserve when Gavrelle was captured, but they relieved the Drake Battalion on the night of 23/24 April. One of these, Leading Seaman Burdon, (A.13), has a very poignant inscription for a sailor who died so far from the sea, 'Anchored on God's Wide Shoreline".

The cemetery has two unknowns, one totally unknown and the other a Royal Marine. The only Great War officer in this cemetery is Lieutenant Austin Cook, RMLI, (D.9).

On 24 September 1917 the RND left the Gavrelle sector to take part in the Third Battle of Ypres, ending up at Passchendaele. The 47th (London) Division took over the Gavrelle Front and the rest of the graves are from this Division

Able Seaman Leslie Burgess, Howe Battalion, and his admiralty Will. Burgess was wounded by shellfire on 28 April 1917, went to the aid post at Marine Trench to be bandaged up, but was mortally wounded when leaving the aid post. One of his relatives has named their house 'Gavrelle' in memory of Leslie Burgess and his comrades.

who were killed in October and November 1917. Most of the graves (most of Row A), are of the 1/Surrey Rifles, who died on 4 November 1917. The War Diary of the 47th Division shows that there was indeed a trench raid on this date, but once again we have the irony of the troops manning the trenches ending up as casualties rather than those actually on the raid. The raid was successful , with all its 194 participants returning safely; however, the battalion garrisoning the trenches on the left of the raid lost nine killed and four wounded from enemy artillery fire during and after the raid. There are eight 1/Surrey Rifles who died on 4 November 1917, plus one killed on 3 November and another who died on 6 November 1917.

There is one Second World War grave in the cemetery, Captain Miller

2/Cameronians (Scottish Rifles), 21 May 1940. During the Arras counter attack, west of Arras, the 2/Cameronians had their HQ in Gavrelle, while helping to hold the flank along the River Scarpe. The War Diaries state that Captain Miller died from 'small arms fire'. There are seven May 1940 graves in Gavrelle Communal Cemetery including two 2/Cameronions. Why Miller is buried in Naval Trench Cemetery and not with the other May 1940 graves is not known. However, Captain Miller has the earliest date, and was killed while Gavrelle was in British hands, so was probably buried by his own men, while the others died on the day (or days after), when the Germans captured the area and were therefore buried by the Germans, or the villagers, in the communal cemetery.

After the Armistice Gavrelle was littered with graves. By 1922 hundreds of graves were exhumed from various small clusters of burials, in and around the village, and all these were concentrated into larger cemeteries, but Naval Trench Cemetery was left. Over 100 metres north west of this cemetery (at B30 c.6.6) was a cluster of twenty-seven graves which were moved to Point-du-Jour Cemetery. As can be seen from the location of the cemetery it is sited in prime agricultural land, so why was this cemetery not moved as well? In general, CWGC cemeteries with over forty burials were to have a Cross of Sacrifice in the cemetery, whilst other clusters of graves under forty were moved to concentration cemeteries. Naval Trench Cemetery is just the tip of the iceberg as regards representing those killed at Gavrelle.

This cemetery does not have a visitors' box for a cemetery register and visitors' book. However, in the near future it is planned to have a visitors' book at the nearby RND Anchor Memorial to compensate for this.

2. ORCHARD DUMP CEMETERY

Orchard Dump Cemetery is the largest CWGC cemetery between Arras and Douai. It has just over 3000 graves, the majority of whom are unknown. This large CWGC cemetery has a thin cemetery register booklet, for every name in the register there are four headstones without a name.

Plan of Orchard Dump cemetery, showing roughly the route of the Walk around Orchard Dump Cemetery.

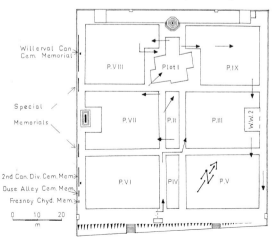

From contemporary aerial photographs the small irregular original plot may be seen (Plot I), and this site, B10 b.80.45 can be plotted on the trench map, page 133, which is inside a rectangle denoting a border. This may have been an orchard, some have suggested

Orchard Dump Cemetery. The irregular plot of original graves can clearly be seen.

the site was an ammunition dump, but the authors have seen no trench map to confirm this. It may have been an old orchard turned into an agricultural dump. The land was given to the CWGC by a widow who had lost her husband in August 1914. This generous gift was responsible for the displacement of hundreds of graves, with most of the graves in this cemetery coming from a 3 kilometre arc, sweeping from Arleux/Fresnoy, Oppy to Gavrelle.

The size of this cemetery, the many unknowns and the displacement of the graves had made it very confusing to the average visitor. About 80% of the graves exhumed at Gavrelle were reburied at Orchard Dump Cemetery, but they are mixed in with the battlefield graves of Oppy Wood and Arleux/Fresnoy. In order to explain this cemetery and show the wealth of information that lies within, there follows a guided walk of it, where interesting graves are pointed out and, by the use of the burial returns, show where originally came from.

A WALK AROUND ORCHARD DUMP CEMETERY

There are two sets of steps up to the cemetery; near one of the steps are four graves, these are original graves and probably were killed near here while using the road. They include a Canadian from the unique formation of Eaton's Motor Machine Gun Battery. This unit was raised and funded by Sir John Graig Eaton (1876-1922), a Toronto merchant and philanthropist.

Continuing north, you come to Plot VI, Captain William Gush, (VI.J.10), 7/RF, 23 April 1917, was originally buried at C19 c.9.7, which is north east of Gavrelle Windmill. Also in this row is Private Morgan, (VI.J.6), 2/RMLI, 28 April 1917, who was also found near the Windmill.

There is a pathway between Plots VI and IV, take this path and on your right is the grave of George Tustin, (VI.G.1), Hood Battalion, 16 July 1917, who was originally buried at Viscount Street, one of thirty-four graves removed from this site. If there had been forty graves, there might have been a small CWGC cemetery near the electricity station, on the boundaries of the communes of Gavrelle and Oppy. Further up, at VI.E.8, is the grave of Private Lee, of 10/East Yorks (Hull Commercials), killed 3 May 1917, who is also from the Viscount Street cluster of graves.

Continue north, but this time take the path between Plots II and III and turn right at Row H. Private Forber, (III.H.2), 1/RMLI is another from Viscount Street. In III.H.1 is Reginald Carter of the London Rifle Brigade, killed when the Germans recaptured Gavrelle on 28 March 1918. Carter came from Peru to join up. The story of the LRB at Gavrelle is told in Chapter Ten of *Gentlemen and Officers* by K.W. Mitchinson. When the Germans attacked Gavrelle on 28 March 1918 one member of the LRB was away from the battalion on a course at the Gas Warfare School at Doullens. His name was Archie Groom, who wrote *Poor Bloody Infantry*. Gavrelle is not mentioned much, because he was not there when the LRB were almost annihilated at the village. There are eight unknown LRB, including one denoting rank, 'Unknown Lance Corporal of the London Rifle Brigade', in this cemetery.

Staying in Row H, walk through Plot II to the next plot. In VII.H.3 is Private Napier RMLI. Next to Napier is an unknown RFC airman, (VII.H.2), who was found at C18 a.9.6 (west of Oppy Wood), and was partially identified as an airman by his buttons and goggles.

Before the end of the path, on your right, is the grave of Private Picket, (II.B.8), 7/Argyll & Sutherland Highlanders, who was found at B24 d.8.1, which is just south of the Gavrelle electricity station. Picket died on 27 August 1918, which was the day after the 51st Division captured Gavrelle in August 1918.

Before the end of the path on your left, in VII.A.12, is Private Hirst RMLI of 190 Brigade MGC, who was found at B23.c.9.7, (near Hill 80). Hirst was probably giving covering fire to the attack on the Windmill on 28 April. He was killed on 29 April 1917, when 1/HAC continued the attack.

Walking out of Plot VII, you will come to the irregular rows of Plot I. These are all original graves, with the exception of two airmen who were brought here many years later from villages behind the German line. Second Lieutenant Claude Madeley came originally from Quiery-La-Motte Communal Cemetery. He flew a Sopwith Camel from 43 Squadron and was shot down on 19 January 1918. Second Lieutenant Pell RFC, flying a Nieuport 17, came from Izel-Les-Equerchin Communal Cemetery. The CWGC said these two graves were moved because of better maintenance efficiency, however, Second Lieutenant E.J. Pascoe RFC was left behind in Izel Communal Cemetery.

Most of the original graves in Plot I are from front line battalions of the 5th Division. In the longest row, Row F of Plot I, there are eight 1/Royal West Kents who died on 9 May 1917. The inscription on Lance Corporal Francis' headstone (I.F.8), reads 'Killed on his 22nd birthday'. On 8 May 1917 the 5th Bavarian Division recaptured Fresnoy and pushed the British back to Arleux, a counter attack by the British 5th Division on 9 May 1917 failed due to heavy shelling of assembling battalions. Row B consists of five 10/Duke of Cornwall's Light Infantry, all died on 7 June 1917. The 10/DCLI were the pioneer battalion of the 2nd Division.

The two rows of graves in front of the Cross of Sacrifice are classified as Rows H and G of Plot I, but these are concentrations and the few named show them to be mostly RND from Gavrelle. The RND continue into Plot VIII, and Private G. Perry, (VIII.C.3), 10/RDF, was found at B25 b.5.4. which is north of Point-du-Jour. He died on 15 April when the RND came up to the line and on their first day probed the area towards Gavrelle, suffering heavy losses.

Going over to Plot IX, walk along Row D. In IX.D.12 is an unknown Captain of the RMLI. There are three RMLI Captains who have their names on the Arras Memorial to the Missing. This body was found near Gavrelle Windmill, two out of the three missing RMLI Captains were in this area at the time of their death. This is another reason why there are so many unknowns at Gavrelle. There were so many killed in this area it was difficult to narrow the possibility by the process of elimination to just one person.

In Row E, in graves 24 and 27, are the graves of two Sub-Lieutenants; Bowles, (25 April 1917), and Banning, (23 April 1917), of the Drake Battalion.

Work your way through the graves, there are many unknown graves there with RND clusters. In this area are headstones with the portcullis of the badge of the Queen's Westminster Rifles, which are usually near to RND graves, showing their Gavrelle connection.

Enter Plot III towards the eastern end. You will notice a group of graves which seem to be spaced at wider intervals than the other graves. These are the Second World War graves. These twenty graves were originally sited in a row flanking the Cross of Sacrifice. The dates show they died from October 1939 to March 1940. They all died of illness or accident during the 'Phoney War'. There was a Casualty Clearing Station (No. 2), at Rouvroy, a few kilometres to the north, and this nearby military cemetery was used to bury the dead.

Around these graves from another war are RND unknown; especially prevalent are the headstones of RMLI unknowns. There are thirty-three RMLI with names, but added to this there are ninety unknown RMLI in this cemetery.

Continue south to the last plot and take the path between the plot and cemetery wall. On the edge of Plot V, the last ten graves of Row A are all either Bedfords, Drakes, RMLI, West Yorks and LRB. Even though they are unknown, from their grouping it suggests that they came from Gavrelle. In Row E there are three unknown LRBs in a row. Further down, on the end of Row F, is Private Meeks of the 15/West Yorks (Leeds Pals), killed on 3 May 1917.

At the end of this plot, by the seat on the wall, is the cemetery visitors book and cemetery register box.

On the western wall of the cemetery are special memorials. The first one is the Fresnoy Churchyard SM to Lieutenant Sinclair RFC who, flying a Nieuport 23 of 40 Squadron, was shot down on 30 March 1917, the day before Bloody April started. He was buried by the Germans, but his grave was lost in the rubble when the Canadians captured Fresnoy a month later.

There is a special memorial to graves lost at Ouse Alley, the main communication trench to Oppy Wood. The six headstones are from the 31st Division, 61st Division and RND. Further along are special memorials to soldiers of the 2nd Canadian Division Cemetery and Willerval Canadian Cemetery, both just north of here, whose graves were destroyed by shellfire.

This has just been a short introduction to this very interesting and important cemetery. No visit or study of Arleux, Fresnoy, Oppy or Gavrelle is complete without a visit to this cemetery. It contains over 2000 graves from the four villages mentioned. If the body of the diarist Private Horace Bruckshaw RMLI, killed at Gavrelle Windmill, was found after the war, it is probably in this cemetery. The same applies to both Lieutenant Jack Harrison VC, 11/East Yorks, killed at Oppy Wood, and Canadian Lieutenant Robert Combe VC, 27/Canadian Battalion, killed north of Fresnoy. Both have no known grave; Harrison has his name on the Arras Memorial to the Missing, and Combe his name on the Canadian Memorial on Vimy Ridge, but they could be under an unknown headstone in Orchard Dump Cemetery.

There are many interesting partially identified unknown graves in this cemetery: unknown 27/Canadian Battalion; unknown airman; unknown British Captain; unknown Lance Corporal Royal Fusiliers; unknown 24th London Regiment; unknown Seaman of the RND; unknown Tyneside Scottish; unknown Sailor of the Anson Battalion; unknown Lieutenant of the RND; unknown Second Lieutenant of the RMLI and so it goes on.

3. ALBUERA CEMETERY

Albuera Cemetery is west of Bailleul, in the protection of the railway embankment of the Arras-Lens railway line. It was made by the 2nd Division which captured the area on 13 April 1917. The introduction in the cemetery register says that the origin of the name is not known, however, it may have its roots from the Peninsular War battle of Albuhera (16 May 1811), which is listed on the battle honours of some British regiments, including the Royal Fusiliers and Middlesex Regiment, who had battalions in the 2nd Division.

This cemetery contains 235 graves, (of which 109 are unknown), in two plots, known simply as North and South. The cemetery register states that 100 graves were concentrated here from the Arras battlefields. The north plot is irregular, suggesting the original cemetery, and the south is uniformly set out, but it has over 100 graves. CWGC documents were consulted, but not the actual burial returns. The only documents found were the 1924 final identification, but, alas, there were no map references. However, there were two unknown graves which were interesting. In South G.1 the unknown soldier was 'found in a tank", and in grave South F.11, the unknown soldier was 'found in tank No. 600". Row D of plot North is mostly unknown with the grave of Private Cafferty, 6/KOYLI, 23 July 1916, (North D.28). So it seems the concentrations are in both plots, but filling in the area between the original cemetery and the railway.

Out of the 109 unknown graves, fourteen were known to be buried among them and they have Special Memorial headstones, (with 'Known to be buried in this cemetery' on), these line the path from the entrance to the Cross of Sacrifice, in two rows.

In this cemetery (as in Naval Trench Cemetery) you can see the change over in late September between the RND and 47th (London) Division, with the latest RND grave being 19th September, and the earliest 47th Division on 1 October 1917 (Corporal LeGrove, 24/London Regiment, North C.19).

In South D.21 is Private Noad of 7/London Regiment, who was killed on 5 October. Private Noad is mentioned in the diaries of Frank Durham, a stretcher bearer of the 47th Division. The book, *The Long Carry* was published in 1970. Durham was working in the Viscount Street area when one of his company, Private Noad, was killed. Durham writes about how monotonous and tiring it was taking Noad's body back by a trench, (presumably along Ouse Alley), to Brigade HQ for burial, with a brief service by a padre.

There are seventeen artillerymen in this cemetery, from 34 Brigade and 84 Brigade, Royal Field Artillery, whose dates of death are on (or just before), the two major attacks of the area, 23 and 28 April 1917. They may have been killed by German counter battery work, when the artillery in this area was providing the preliminary bombardment for these attacks.

Most of the graves here are from the RND and 31st Division, who were protecting the line from Oppy Wood to Gavrelle. The 190 Brigade of the RND, the 'Landlubbers' are well represented here. These were the army battalions in the RND: 1/HAC, 4/Bedfords, 7/RF and 10 Royal Dublin Fusiliers.

The 31st Division is also represented in this cemetery. Many headstones have the Tiger badge of the York and Lancaster Regiment, the Star of the West Yorkshire Regiment and the Sphinx of 11/East Lancashire Regiment (Accrington Pals). Their dates include the 3 May attack, and even four dated 27 and 29 June, 1917, the days before and after the successful attack on Cardona Trench. The day with the most 31st Division casualties is 15 May 1917, when the trench south of Oppy Wood was attacked, and there were many casualties due to uncut wire.

There is one RFC member, Air Mechanic Second Class Hickling (South C.1). He crashed in a BE2c flying over Fresnoy. The pilot, Second Lieutenant Owen died of wounds and is in St Catherine Cemetery (now a suburb of Arras), which would suggest they crashed just behind the British lines. Hickling was shot down on 7 May 1917, the same day Albert Ball died near Lens, and Mick Mannock shot down his first (confirmed) enemy plane over nearby Quiety-la-Motte. Mannock went on to become the highest scoring British air ace of the war.

This cemetery also contains one German artilleryman, Willy Garland, 6/Battalion, 60/Regiment Field Artillery. His CWGC headstone states he died on 16 March 1919. After the war there was a German prisoner of war camp at Vitry-en-Artois, and they were employed in clearing debris from the Arras battlefield. There is a high probability that Willy died accidentally from battlefield ordnance and was buried in the nearest cemetery, but there are other possible reasons for this unique headstone in this cemetery.

Out of the ten cemeteries on this tour, this is possibly the least easy to reach. The cobbled stone lane is rather bone shaking, and there is only the side of a bank for parking, not to mention trying to turn around. This cemetery was located here to get some protection from shells overhead, using the railway embankment for shelter. It was a 'long carry' for Frank Durham to bring his dead comrade to this spot to be buried, but this secluded cemetery is worth the effort of a visit.

Map 46: Trench Map showing location of Albuera Cemetery (B21 a 6.7). Note the communication trench 'Ouse Alley' just north of the Cemetery.

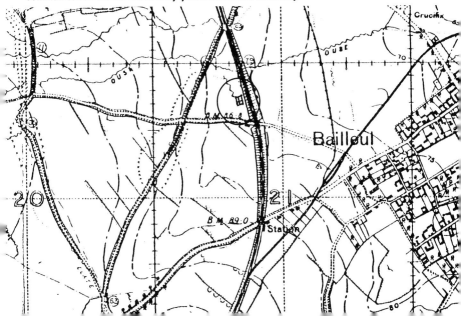

4. BAILLEUL ROAD EAST CEMETERY

Bailleul Road East Cemetery lies in the apex of the triangle created by a farm lane branching off the D919. This area was captured by the Northumberland Fusiliers of the 34th Division on 9 April 1917, and their graves make up the first few rows of Plot I. The whole of this plot are original burials, ending with August 1918 graves, when the area was recaptured.

Colour Sergeant Fredrick Wellard CH/130 1/Royal Marine Light Infantry, RN (63 Division, killed in action in the front l trenches at Gavrelle, 16 August 1917.

Photographs of Wellard, and his origi wooden Cross, and letter to his wife, Wellard's Commanding Officer giving information about how he died. Wellard is n buried in Bailleul Road East Cemetery.

Left: Wellard's great-great-grandson, Th Pilten, at the headstone on the 8 anniversary of Wellard's death, 16 August 19

The roughly chronological order of the graves shows which battalions were here and when. On 26 June 1917 1/HAC left the RND and were replaced by the Artists' Rifles, and in this plot there are graves of 1/HAC up to plot N, and Artists' Rifles from plot 0.

Even though this cemetery, and nearby Dressing Station, were a few kilometres from the Front Line, and contain many who died of wounds, nevertheless, many killed at Gavrelle were taken to this cemetery by their comrades to be buried. Colour Sergeant Major Frederick Wellard, 1/RMLI (T.N.15), was killed instantly at Gavrelle by a German pineapple grenade on 16 August 1917. Wellard was in the trenches talking to Sergeant Blackstock, who was wounded; the latter's grave is at Aubigny Cemetery, east of Arras, which had a nearby Casualty Clearing Station.

Lance Corporal Everest 1/RMLI (I.P.13), was killed at Gavrelle on 3rd September 1917 by a sniper. Everest enlisted on 10 November 1915 at Brighton.

There are eleven pioneers of the RND, the 14/Worcester Regiment, in this plot. The 317 Brigade RFA were the RND's artillery, and they too are represented in Plot I.

All the other graves in the other plots are mostly from other areas; from south of the Scarpe, from north of Lens, and many more from further afield on the Western Front.

Plot II contains some 1914 graves from the 'race to the open flank' battles north of Lens. Most of these are from 1/Highland Light Infantry. Lieutenant Guthrie Smith, 1/HLI (II.N.7), son of Major General Sir Herbert Guthrie Smith, KGB, was killed at Festubert on 20 December 1914.

The graves even come from far south, such as Second Lieutenant Thomas Davies, (II.G.7) 2/RWF, 27 May 1917. His grave came from near Fontaine-les-Crosilles. Captain J.C. Dunn, in *The War the Infantry Knew*, describes the attack on Tunnel Trench made by 2/RWF. The battalion had ten officers and 155 other ranks casualties, about half killed, on 27 May 1917.

The only RFC casualty in this cemetery is Second Lieutenant Lawledge RFC, (II.I.23) who, flying a Sopwith Strutter, was shot down on 10 October 1916, and was originally buried in Lagnicourt German Cemetery.

In Plot III there are many Australians who chased the Germans to the Hindenburg Line during March 1917. One of them seems to have German roots, Robert Oscar von Stieglitz, 26/Australian Battalion, (III.C.14), killed on 26 March 1917. This battalion was fighting in front of Lagnicourt, where Captain Percy Cherry, 26/Australian, was awarded the VC. Cherry was also killed on the 26 March 1917, but is buried in Quéant Road Cemetery, not far from Lagnicourt.

In Row C graves 28-29 are two Australians, both found in the same place at Lagnicourt, (57c, C24 d.7.9). Sergeant Lennon was identified by his disc, but the other Australian could not be identified despite personal possessions in his pockets, including part of a letter.

In Plot IV are a few 7/Dragoon Guards killed on 1 December 1917, who were dismounted cavalry and fighting near Cambrai during the German counter attack at the Battle of Cambrai.

Plot V contains the sixty-nine graves from Northumberland Cemetery (H1 a 90.15). The graves in this plot have similar dates and regiments as those in Sunken Road Cemetery, the two cemeteries were originally half a kilometre apart. In this plot is the most famous grave here, the artist and poet Isaac Rosenberg 1/KORL, killed 1 April 1918. His grave is unusual, because he was identified in a group. Rosenberg's headstone has 'Buried Near this Spot', as does five other of his comrades: Privates Fred Lord, James O'Boyle, David Pritchard, Robert Williams, and Lance Corporal Patrick O'Donovan. Rosenberg's remains could be under any one of these headstones.

Northumberland Cemetery had over the forty minimum graves, and its location was on the maps of the earlier cemetery registers, which shows that its concentration into this cemetery was a very late decision. Most cemeteries were moved because of problems about access or problems with the owner of the land. However, there could be other reasons. Rosenberg's poems were not published until the mid-1920s, then he started to get famous, which could have resulted in creating more pressure on the authorities to find his grave. If they were going to have to dig up Northumberland Cemetery to look for his grave among the unknowns, they might as well have moved the complete cemetery, therefore saving future maintenance costs. The question of why Northumberland Cemetery was moved at such a late date still remains unanswered.

The concentrated graves which have come from the furthest distance are three unknowns from Gommecourt, and even an unknown from the Warwickshire Regiment (IV.C.4), who was buried at 57c X21 d 95.80, which is Pigeon Ravine, near Epehy, 40 kilometres away to the south west.

Also in this cemetery is a set of examples showing errors in the cemetery registers. After the war, the next of kin were sent Final Verification forms, to check details, and add extra information, e.g. age, parents, address etc. Some of these forms were never sent back, and some were never even received. Those names in the register which have just the basic information had no Final Verification form sent back. Those which have the extra information do so because the family sent back the form; however, because this information was supplied by the family it can be subjective.

Private Obee 22/NF (Tyneside Scottish), 9 April 1917, has 'Killed in action at Hill 60", in the cemetery register. Corporal Wrightson, 3/South African Infantry, 9 April 1917, has 'Killed in action Delville Wood' written on the cemetery register. Both of these soldiers are in Plot I, both died on the first day of the Battle of Arras, not far from this cemetery, but the families have put down the more well known battles in which their regiments had fought in. These battles were much publicised in the newspapers of the day.

5. ST LAURENT-BLANGY GERMAN CEMETERY

Most people reading this guide will be of British/Commonwealth origin, and many of us have subconscious national cultural beliefs that make us uncomfortable in German war cemeteries. They are often dismissed as being too dark, stark and sombre. It is hoped that this introduction to the cemetery will help you appreciate and understand German war cemeteries.

The Germans were the vanquished, so little land was set aside for German cemeteries. This has resulted in fewer cemeteries compared with the Allies, but these cemeteries contain many more war dead. The Germans also believe in mass burial, these are called *Kamradengräber*, where comrades are buried together, individual comrades mixed to make a greater whole. All large German cemeteries can be divided into individual and mass graves. There are two large German cemeteries in the Arras area.

Neuville-St. Vaast German Cemetery	graves	36793
	mass graves	8040
St Laurent-Blangy German Cemetery	graves	7022
	mass graves	24670

Neuville-St Vaast German Cemetery, sited north of Arras on the old 'Labyrinth' battlefield, is one of the largest German cemeteries on the Western Front. Notice that St Laurent-Blangy German Cemetery, although it is smaller, contains many more remains in its *Kamradengräber*, and is sited north east of Arras.

As pointed out in the first chapter, there was a large German cemetery in Gavrelle during the war. This cemetery was destroyed in the capture of Gavrelle in April 1917, but with the numerous counter attacks, and the costly recapture in March 1918, thousands more Germans were added to the soil of the commune of Gavrelle. Where are all these Germans now?

The authors wrote to the German War Graves Commission, *Volksdund Deutsche Kriegsgräberforsorge*, about the fate of the graves in the destroyed cemetery at Gavrelle. The VDK wrote back to say, that unfortunately most of their records were destroyed during the bombing of the Second World War, but they were probably taken to Neuville-St Vaast or St Laurent-Blangy German Cemeteries. There were many more German cemeteries in the eastern part of Arras besides Gavrelle, and most of these would have been destroyed, so that when the exhumation was attempted, it would have been easier to dig up the cemetery en masse, and transport it to a *Kamradengräber*. The names would have been taken from German records of the original cemetery, and some people believe this is why the *Kamradengräber* in this vast cemetery contains the remains of thousands more Germans than Neuville-St Vaast German Cemetery, as it contains the remains of the German cemeteries from Vitry, Biache, Gavrelle, etc.

It is convenient to have a CWGC cemetery near to a German cemetery, so that the two cultural approaches may be compared. The first difference you can see, is the greater number of trees in the German cemetery. CWGC cemeteries are designed to be like an English country garden with flowers, lawns and a few trees. The German cemeteries are designed on the mythical grove, the spiritual shadiness, literally a black forest. The trees are usually everlasting evergreen, with a few oaks, as this is a Germanic symbol for strength. In the English garden CWGC cemeteries, neat boundaries and straight lanes are the rule.

This is not the case in German cemeteries, and sometimes winding lanes can be found in their cemeteries.

The main difference between the two types of cemeteries are flowers. The English garden influence has already been explained, added to this, another flower, the poppy became the symbol of remembrance. If we look at this from the Germanic angle, flowers only last a short time (especially those picked), then they die. The theme in a German cemetery is perpetual life. Flowers die, but wreathes made of fir cones and moss last for years, even the trees last for generations. A CWGC cemetery cannot have many trees as the white headstones would soon be slimy green with growth from the shade, what better colour than black or grey for the shaded groves of German cemeteries.

Now you can see a German cemetery through German eyes, maybe it will not be so gloomy and dark. You might not agree with all the analysis, however, visiting the cemetery and looking at it in a different light, it may not seem so uncomfortable, and you will benefit from your visit.

St Laurent-Blangy Cemetery is set in a little valley known as 'Wire Valley' during the war. Most of this cemetery was covered in rows of barbed wire protecting the railway cutting, whose sides were riddled with dugouts. The high ground near the railway was part of Bois de la Maison Blanche and probably where the original cemetery was.

The cemetery can be divided into three parts, front and back, with the *Kamradengräber* in between. At the entrance there are two thick cemetery registers, unfortunately they only have name, rank, unit, and date of death, and no further information as in the CWGC cemetery registers. The first part of the cemetery is unusually spacious. See if you can find an oak tree, and if there are any evergreen cone wreathes on the crosses. On the northern side, near the *Kamradengräber*, is a patch of 1919 and 1920 graves, probably from the post war PoW camps in the area. One wonders how many died of Spanish Flu, after thinking themselves lucky to survive the war, only to be buried with their comrades who fell in the war.

Stretching across the cemetery is the *Kamradengräber*, note how raised it is. There is a path running along the top, with bronze sheets either side with names of the German soldiers whose remains are said to be here. You might be lucky to see a name that has been scratched with a coin to highlight it, made to stand out from the rest, by a visiting relative.

Behind the *Kamradengräber* the land rises, and there are more German graves, right up to the railway cutting. Behind a wire fence the Arras-Lens railway line lies, several metres down, showing the protection given during the war, and what an excellent tank trap this railway cutting was. This area and the wood across the railway was Bois de la Maison Blanche, (not to be confused with La Maison Blanche which was about a kilometre west of here). When captured by the British, this area would have been the Piccadilly Circus of the 'behind the lines' area of the Gavrelle Sector; with dugouts, aid posts, supply dumps, troops moving up to Gavrelle, and troops coming back, sometimes with PoWs, and sometimes with their dead comrades to be buried. It is a very lonely and quiet place today, a wooded garden city with a permanent population of nearly 32000.

To understand and appreciate the Germans on the Western Front more, there are two books we recommend, *Victory Must Be Ours*, and *Fallen Soldiers*. Full details may be found in the Bibliography.

6. POINT-DU-JOUR CEMETERY

Point-du-Jour is on high ground at the toe of Vimy Ridge. This strategic position once had a house, some sources say a farm. The Germans made a strongpoint here. Point-du-Jour was on the boundary of the 34th and 9th Divisions, and was captured on the first day of the Battle of Arras, 9 April 1917. It was from this position that the RND attacked Gavrelle on 23 April 1917. It was this strongpoint that helped to halt the German advance of March and April 1918.

Note the little hollow in which the cemetery lies, which would have provided some protection, despite being sited on high ground. This cemetery contains 738 graves (including some from 1940), and just over half, (372) are unknown. The original graves numbered eighty-two, now most of Plot I, but the cemetery was greatly enlarged after the Armistice from graves on the Arras Battlefield and, as will be shown, from much further afield.

There was another small cemetery nearby and this was concentrated into this cemetery along with other clusters of graves at Effie Trench Fampoux, and two other sites from the coalmining areas to the north. The cemetery closest to Gavrelle, and now part of Point-du-Jour, was Lonely House Cemetery, which was half way between Point-du-Jour and Gavrelle.

The original graves from the cemetery can be seen in the slightly irregular rows of A to G. However, this is just a general rule, as other graves have been added to some rows. Lieutenant William Durant (I.A.6), New Zealand Engineers, and nine other NZ Tunnelers went on a disastrous trench raid on 14 September 1916 with a Cheshire battalion. The job of the engineers was to lay demolition charges in the German position. Lieutenant Durant was one of the few who ever reached the German trenches, in an action that took place a few kilometres down the road to Arras.

The 1917 graves naturally start with the Scots and South Africans of the 9th Division, who captured Point-du-Jour on the first day of the Battle of Arras. The rows follow the usual flow of battalions who fought here, with the dates of death showing when in the area, ending with the casualties of the German March 1918 Offensive.

There were forty-seven French graves, but forty-four unknown graves were exhumed after the war, presumably to go in to the Ossuary at Notre Dame de Lorette (another nationality that believes in mass burials). Collecting French graves and remains at Notre Dame de Lorette has made the site very impressive, but it has left a large gap in this cemetery. One of the three French graves left behind is very interesting. Unusually it has a CWCG headstone, which states that Sergeant-Major Maurice de Vernot of the 360th Infantry Regiment fell in action in front of Gavrelle on 2 October 1914. Why should de Vernot have a CWGC headstone, and the other two French crosses? The information written on the headstone would not be able to fit on a French cross, but is this the reason, or just the consequence?

One thing this average size CWGC cemetery is not short of is officers, both named and partially unknown. This includes two high ranking officers Lieutenant-Colonel SAVAGE-ARMSTRONG, II.E.12, 11/Warwicks, 112 Brigade, 37 Division, was originally of the 1/South Staffords, but was commanding the 11/Warwicks when killed on 23 April 1917. His details in the cemetery register lists an impressive war record. In III.C.2 is the grave of Lieutenant Colonel Charles BURKE, DSO, East Lancs, who was killed on 9 April 1917. His details in the cemetery register say 'Went to France in August 1914 in command of No. 2 Squadron, Royal Flying Corps".

In III.G.4 is the grave of Lieutenant Gerald Tamplin, Hood Battalion who died on 23rd April 1917 in Gavrelle, the same shell also killing Lieutenant James Morrison, who has no known grave, and is commemorated on the Arras Memorial to the Missing. However, both officers have their name on the Hood Cross in Gavrelle Church.

The unknown officers in this cemetery are also interesting. There are two sets of unknown British officers and two unknown Lieutenants, and one headstone to an unknown Second Lieutenant of the Lancashire Fusiliers. The most well known missing of this rank and regiment killed in this area is Bernard Cassidy VC. There are a few second lieutenants of the Lancashire Fusiliers in the Memorial Register of the Arras missing.

The burial returns of Private J. Smith, III.E.6. 50/MGC, killed on 16 May 1917, shows he was originally buried on Hyderabad Redoubt. Able Seaman Henry Hutchison IV.E.18, Nelson Battalion, killed on 23 April 19197 was originally buried at C25 a.3.3, in a garden west of the Mayor's house in Gavrelle. Found with the body was a calico wrapping with an address, his pay book and a 'Nelson' cap tally.

There are two RFC airmen in this cemetery, but they both come from the Cambrai area. Second Lieutenant Godfrey, IV.E.12, was killed on 23 September 1916 whilst flying a Martinsyde G100 and was brought from Masnières Churchyard. Second Lieutenant Coxe, II.A.13, was flying a BE2c and died on 1 July 1916, reported shot down near Cambrai.

To continue the Cambrai/Masnières connection, there are twenty-four Royal Guernsey Light Infantry (both known and partially known) in this cemetery, all of whom died 1 December 1917. History show that they were with the 29th Division during the Battle of Cambrai, during the German counter attack. The burial returns confirm they all came from a small burial ground south west of Masnières, (57B G26 c.9.3). It seems those studying the casualties of the Battle of Cambrai should certainly include an examination of the cemeteries around Arras!

Along the eastern wall are Special Memorial headstones to sixteen soldiers known to be buried in this cemetery. Along the western wall are special memorials to two known to be buried at Effie Trench Cemetery and four known to be buried at Lonely House Cemetery, but their graves could not be found. The four Lonely House Special Memorials are all 9/North Staffs killed on 26 April 1917. The 9/North Staffs were the pioneers of the 37th Division. The Official History states that after the heavy casualties of the 23 April attack, the

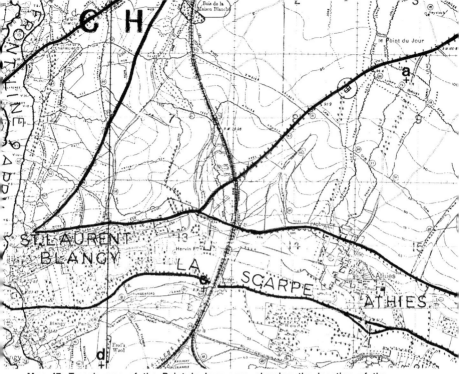

Map 47: Trench map of the Point-du-Jour area, showing the location of the Cemetery, and the original Front Line. The original location of graves in the cemetery have been marked with a cross. 'a' is the original grave site of Lieutenant Colonel Savage-Armstrong (H9 a 8.6.), 'b' marks the site of the grave of the unknown Second Lieutenant of the Lancashire Fusiliers, (H9. d 9.9). At 'c' was found the grave of the New Zealander Lieutenant William Durant, (H13 d 5.3), on his cross was written, 'Nier Ruhen vier Tapfere Englander'. At 'd' near Fred's Wood was found the grave of Private Hanlon 7/8 KOSB, 15th Division, (G24 b 9.1).

pioneers were sent up to the Front Line to help against expected German counter attacks.

In the cemetery register it states that twenty-five sailors, soldiers and marines were concentrated here from Lonely House Cemetery. The burial returns show that some, maybe all, are in Row B of Plot III. These include Private Gray, RMLI, III.B.1; Unknown RND, III.B.10; and Driver Read, V/31st Heavy Trench Mortar Battery, RFA, 14 May 1917, III.B.13.

Another cluster of graves are the twenty-seven from near Naval Trench Cemetery. These include Able Seamen Roach, Tull and Twittey, and Leading Seaman Nicol, all of whom are in Row E of Plot III.

The year 1918 is well represented here with Queen's Westminster Rifles and 1/KOLR, (Isaac Rosenberg's Battalion), from 28 March German attack.

There are three 4/Green Howards (Yorkshire Regiment) 1940 graves near the shelter. Two of them are joint graves with one headstone. This battalion were holding the River Scarpe flank east of Arras, when the Arras counter attack was taking place west of Arras on 21 May 1940.

7. CHILI TRENCH CEMETERY

Chili Trench Cemetery is sited in the commune of Gavrelle, near the border with the commune of Fampoux. It gets its name from a communication tranch, Chili Avenue, that ran west to east, just north of the cemetery. It contains 196 graves, seventeen are unknown and eighty-six are represented by Special Memorials. The cemetery was started by the 37th Division and their graves dominate the cemetery.

37th DIVISION

63 BDE: 8/Lincolnshire, 8/SLI, 4/Middlesex, 10/York & Lancs
111 BDE: 10/RF, 13/RF, 13/KRRC, 13/Rifle Brigade
112 BDE: 11/Warwickshire, 6/Bedfords, 8/East Lancs, 10/Loyal North Lancs

On 23 April and again on 29 April the 37th Division attacked towards Greenland Hill and the area north, which is roughly where the two motorways interchange to the east. The 11/RF and the 13/RF are particularly numerous, as they attacked the field directly east of the cemetery. There is a Special Memorial headstone to Second Lieutenant Osborne 13/KRRC (SM 16), killed in action on 23 April 1917. The 13/KRRC were on the extreme left flank, south of Gavrelle, linking up with the Drake Battalion of the RND.

Unusually, all the original graves only span a few weeks of April and May. The casualties end when the Battle of Arras ends (mid-May). Presumably, when the Front Line stabilised, it was thought better to bury casualties further back, in cemeteries like Sunken Road and Northumberland.

This is a battlefield cemetery and not a concentration cemetery, but it does have four concentrations which were reburied here in 1935 (last four graves in Row E). They are two airmen and two soldiers, from the village of Monchecourt, south east of Douai. This village was well behind the German lines, so the soldiers probably died of wounds while prisoners of war. The two airmen of 62 Squadron RAF were reported shot down near Cambrai on 15 September 1918. In 'Bloody April' in 1917 the RFC sustained considerable casualties. The RAF came into being on 1 April 1918, but September 1918 was also a month of exceptional casualties and is generally known as 'Black September'. Two RAF casualties of Black September now rest in this cemetery, but they are not the only RAF here.

There is one 1940 grave in this cemetery. On 19 May 1940 Flying Officer David Bury was flying a Hurricane of 111 Squadron when he crashed into an electricity pylon near the cemetery, while being chased by a Messerschmitt 109. He was a former head boy at Eton College.

Flying with Bury was Pilot Officer Iain Moorhead who was also involved in a dog fight over Gavrelle/Vitry, but Moorhead went on to crash south west of Arras and is the only CWGC grave in Sains-les-Marquion Churchyard.

David Bury was born in 1915 and his father, Captain Edmond Bury, 11/KRRC, was in the trenches near Armentiers and died on 5 December 1915, and is buried in Rue-Petillion Military Cemetery. A father and son, both killed in France in different wars and lying only 36 kilometres apart, R.I.P.

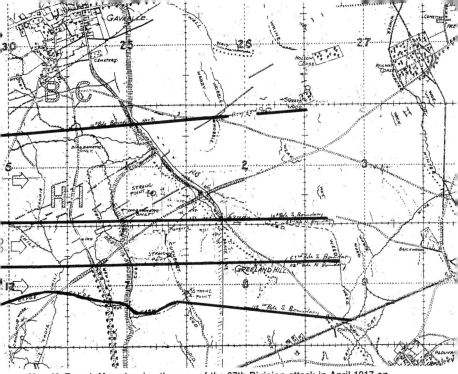

Map 48: Trench Map showing the area of the 37th Division attack in April 1917 on Greenland Hill, south of Gavrelle. The boundaries of the three Brigades are marked along with the boundaries of the RND and 37th Division. The line of small dashes indicates the 'Green Line' objective.

8. SUNKEN ROAD CEMETERY

Sunken Road cemetery has 196 graves, of which twenty-six are unidentified, and there are sixteen Special Memorial headstones to those buried here but whose graves were lost due to shell fire. The siting of the cemetery is very curious, as it is on the exposed eastern bank of Sunken Road.

This area was captured by the 4th Division, who managed to capture Hyderabad Redoubt.

There are thirteen graves from the attack of 3 May 1917. They are from 5/Camerons, 9/Camerons, 8/Black Watch. 11/Royal Scots, of the 9th (Scottish) Division, and 2/Essex of the 4th Division.

There are two Tynside Scottish here from the attack on Greenland Hill on 5 June 1917: Private Allan, 20/NF (Special Memorial A8) and Lance Corporal Preston, 22/NF (I.D. 17).

Looking through the register, there are many graves here for mid-1917, from the 17th Division, (10/Sherwood Foresters, 8/South Staffs, 12/Manchesters, 7/Yorkshires, 6/Dorsets, 3/4 Royal West Kents). The 17th Division consisted of 50, 51 and 52 Brigades and the same numbers were applied to the Division's Machine Gun Companies, and they, too, are represented in this cemetery.

In I.C. 25 is the grave of Private Ormerod of the Tank Corps, who died on 5

October 1917; not only is he the only tank crew in this cemetery, and in the area, but 'Soldiers Died in the Great War' shows that he is the only member of the Tank Corps to die on 5 October 1917.

The end of 1917 is represented by battalions of the 61st Division, and there are a group of graves of the 1/5Duke of Cornwall's Light Infantry, the 61st Division's pioneers, all killed on 27 October 1917.

There are also some Guardsmen from early 1918. There are all from the Scots and Grenadier Guards, and presumably this was their sector of the line. The Welsh Guards held the sector next to the River Scarpe.

There are about 25 unknowns in this cemetery, the partially unknown include seven from the Rifle Brigade, one Royal Engineer, one York and Lancs, and one 'A Welsh Soldier of the Great War'.

Looking south towards Fampoux on the horizon is Monchy-le-Preux. The large white building on the right marks the industrial estate where archaeologists looking for Roman remains found the graves of twenty-seven British soldiers in December 1996 (see photograph on page 157). The sunken road marks the limit of the German March 1918 offensive in this area, responsible for the loss of many grave markers. There are still graves out there waiting to be discovered.

9. FAMPOUX BRITISH CEMETERY

This battlefield cemetery has no graves from Gavrelle, but does contain many who died on their way to Hyderabad Redoubt. In the introduction of the cemetery register it states that the cemetery was at one time called Helena Trench Cemetery, but finding this name on trench maps is not easy. Many trenches changed their names during the war and trenches were abandoned, and new trenches dug over four years of trench warfare. Effie Trench ran from Point-du-Jour, alongside this cemetery and then on to Fampoux. Also, this cemetery is just north of the old German 'third line of defence' trench system. The cemetery register states the cemetery was started by troops from the 4th and 34th Divisions when the area was captured on the first day of the Battle of Arras. The 4th Division has the most graves in this cemetery, which makes up nearly half of the total of 110 known, and also has eight unknown graves.

After the Armistice, the four rows of graves extended nearer to the road, but with the construction of the perimeter wall, ten graves were moved to form Row E. This battlefield cemetery was in the area of the 9th Division attack, and contains Scottish and South African troops from this Division. The 4th Division leapfrogged through this area and, as stated before, they have the most graves of any Division in the Cemetery. The 4th Dvision has also the last casualty in this cemetery, killed 5th April 1918, when the 4th Division was once more in the area, to stop the German 28 March Offensive.

Other divisions are represented here, with a few graves from the 51st, 34th, 17th and 12th Divisions. In early 1918 the Guards Division took over the Front Line, and there are ten Guardsmen of the Coldstream and Scots Guards, casualties from late January to early March 1918.

There is one cavalryman, Private Baker (B.48), in this cemetery. 5/Dragoon

Guards came up through Fampoux to the Front Line on 10 April 1917, but the Germans had reinforced the position, so there was no chance of a breakthrough, so they trundled back to Arras through a snowstorm. They suffered a handful of casualties, one of whom was buried in this cemetery.

In C.4 is the grave of twenty-one year old Guardsman George Young. The cemetery register says he was 'a gardener employed by the Earl of Rosebery at Dalmeny". The Dalmeny Estate is north west of Edinburgh. This young Scotsman now rests in a CWGC 'English Garden' near Fampoux.

10. BROWN'S COPSE CEMETERY

Brown Copse Cemetery lies on the communal border between Fampoux and Roeux, being just inside the commune of Roeux. It contains graves of nearly 2000 soldiers, mainly those killed while attacking Roeux, but after the war 850 graves were concentrated here from surrounding areas, including many from Greenland Hill and south of Gavrelle.

During the battle of Arras the numerous attacks on Roeux had resulted in the area between Fampoux and Roeux being littered with hundreds of bodies. At the start of the summer, when the weather was getting warmer and the Front Line had stabilised, it was decided to bury the dead. During the War there was a small copse known as Bois Rossignol, Nightingale Wood, east of the original plots. It seems the cemetery was sited here because, being so close to the Front Line, the copse would provide some protection. This copse was known to the British as Brown's Copse, hence the name of the cemetery; however, the name seldom appears on trench maps.

During the summer of 1917 just over 1000 graves were brought here to be buried, and they are now plots I-III and includes the grave of Lieutenant Donald Mackintosh VC of 2/Seaforths (II.C.49). Mackintosh was one of those who attacked Roeux on 11 April 1917 from where the Seaforths Celtic Cross Memorial is sited today. There are just over 100 named 2/Seaforths in these plots, who died with Mackintosh on that 11 April attack.

Since Plots I-III were brought in during the war, there are no burial returns to know their original location, all that is known, is it was not far from this site. There is one RFC in these plots, that of Lieutenant Fuller RFC (III.D.13), who crashed on 17 May 1917 at H24 b, which is under a kilometre away, to the western side of Mount Pleasant Hill.

These plots contain many headstones, shared by two or more soldiers, showing that the bodies were so close together that they were unfortunately mixed when exhumed. An above average number of the unknown graves are partially identified.

Plot IV is also an original plot, but were buried after the cemetery was established, and therefore are buried in roughly chronological order. Plot IV was also sited to benefit from the shelter of the copse. The earliest graves in this plot are from mid-June, which indicates when the previous plots were brought in, and when this plot was started. Plot IV shows the battalions which were at this Front Line from June 1917 to early 1918. The last graves are from the Guards Division, who were here in early 1918. In this plot are many graves

179

of the 2/6Warwicks of the 61st Division, killed on 24 September 1917. Something seems to have been going on that day near this cemetery, a trench raid?

The rest of the plots were made after the Armistice, filling in the space between the original plots and the access lane. The cemetery register gives the names of two burial sites concentrated here, that of Seaforth Cemetery, Roeux, which had eighteen British soldiers, and twenty-one 6/Seaforths who died capturing the area in late 1918. The other site given is Vitry-en-Artois Communal Cemetery and German Extension, which contained seventeen British who presumably died of wounds while prisoners of war, or were aircrew of the RFC.

Chief Petty Officer Webster, Drake Battalion, (VII.D.19), was found at Gavrelle, C25 c.2.3. (west of the allotments), and was killed on 23 April 1917, when the Drake Battalion captured south Gavrelle. The other RND in this cemetery is 'Unknown soldier of the RND' (V.C.2); why this grave is recorded as a soldier, and not a seaman is not known. The badge on the headstone is that of the Admiralty Fouled Anchor, which is usually on the naval battalions of the RND headstones. As explained before, there are exceptions to every rule, and some headstones in cemeteries say 'A Sailor', and some 'A Seaman' when referring to someone from the naval battalions of the RND. In *Courage Remembered*, (the story behind the construction and maintenance of the Commonwealth's military cemeteries and memorials), states that 'a sailor' is for armed naval forces, and 'a seaman' for merchant navies, but it seems it depends upon who was doing the records at the time.

Near the west wall are Special Memorials, two are from Vitry-en-Artois, and six are general Special Memorial headstones, including Private Teale 15/West Yorks, 3 May 1917 (SM.6). Next to Teale is the SM headstone to Major Harvey-Kelly DSO, shot down 29 April 1917 by the German Ace, Oberleutnant Kurt Wolff. Wolff went on to shoot down another two planes that day, one of which crashed west of Gavrelle.

The burial returns show that Greenland Hill was covered in graves, and these were moved to this cemetery, but alas most of them are unknown. In V.A.3 is the grave of Private Mulholland 22/NF (Tyneside Scottish), 5 June 1917. For every identified Tyneside Scottish headstone in this cemetery, there are three or four unknown Tyneside Scottish.

There are 856 unknown graves here, some of the interesting partially unknowns are: an unknown sergeant of the Gordon Highlanders, 29 May 1917; an unknown captain, 4/South African Infantry, 26 May 1917; an unknown second lieutenant, Gordon Highlanders, 13 May 1917; an unknown sergeant, Somerset Light Infantry, 13 May 1917; unknown officer, Essex Regiment; an unknown corporal, Gordon Highlanders, 19 May 1917, and so on.

Access to this cemetery is down a lane. This lane originally went from Fampoux to Roeux, but in the early 1990s, when the TGV was constructed, half the Roeux side of the lane was swallowed up by the new railtrack, so there is now no drive through and one must turn around at the cemetery entrance, which could be difficult for large cars.

Chapter Ten

RECENT MEMORIALS IN GAVRELLE

In the 1990s two memorials were built in Gavrelle, the RND Anchor Monument and a memorial to Gavrelle's most famous son, Pierre Carpentier. This chapter explains the story behind these two recent monuments in Gavrelle, one First World War and one Second World War.

THE RND ANCHOR MEMORIAL

The main action at Gavrelle was its capture by the RND in April 1917, however, a memorial to this action was not erected until 75 years later. Why was this? The main reason was the RND was a victim of its own success during the Great War. It was the other famous actions of the RND (e.g. Gallipoli 1915, the Ancre 1916 and Passchendaele 1917), that overshadowed the action at Gavrelle, and even the Battle of Arras (apart from the capture of Vimy Ridge) was slipping away into obscurity. There is a large obelisk type RND monument on the Ancre, but this is dedicated to the actions of the Ancre 1916, whilst the unit badges are only cap size, a size change was needed to be incorporated in the new monument.

In the late 1980s a small group of individuals decided to build a memorial to the capture of Gavrelle by the RND. The memorial consists of a three ton anchor (the RND Divisional badge) set in a bombed-out building, which represented the destroyed village. This monument is, possibly, the only monument on the Western Front that is dedicated both to those who fought

The Anchor being lifted into position on the monument at Gavrelle. (1990)

here and also to the destruction of a village. This memorial was designed by one of the authors, who freely admits to the influence of the American sculptor and architect, James Wine. During the 1970s Wine produced buildings with features of peeling facades and cascading bricks which made his buildings look as though they had suffered a nuclear attack or earthquake. The Anchor looks as though it is growing out of the building, and the half-walls and tumble-down brickwork show the destruction of the village. This design breaks away from conventional memorials, and takes into account maintenance costs and other future expenses. The design incorporates an anti-vandalism element, symbolically, it looks as though it is already vandalised.

The other aspect of the Anchor memorial lies in the use of materials. Gavrelle was constructed mostly of red bricks (the combatants fighting in the village were covered in red brick dust), so it was imperative that the monument was constructed with local red bricks. The nearby monuments of the 9th (Scottish) Division Memorial and the Seathforth Highlanders' Celtic Cross are both made from imported granite from Scotland.

The three ton anchor is (unsurprisingly) not local, and was donated by Her Majesty's Salvage and Mooring Depot at Pembroke Dock. This anchor was dragged up from Milford Haven, lost by a nineteenth century naval ship. Besides donating this find, the Depot also sandblasted the crustaceans and rust off, and red-leaded the anchor.

The anchor was transported from Pembroke Dock to Gavrelle in the spring of 1989 by a party of Royal Marines, led by Lieutenant R.M. Tonner RM and Marines, Rawlinson, Reeves, Ripley and Slatter. The five RMs were asked to sign the Fund logo and the Memorial Fund produced 'Royal Marine Anchor Transport Team' 'T' shirts, and these were presented to the five Royal Marines.

Acquiring the land was delayed by bureaucratic red tape and the anchor was temporarily placed in the forecourt of Hotel Le Manoir for nearly a year. When the site was finally secured, the monument was built in the summer of 1990 and the anchor was taken from the 'mayor's house' to the monument, and the tumble-down brickwork added. The commune of Gavrelle provided the flagpoles.

Battlefield debris has been incorporated in the brickwork. All these items were found within walking distance of the monument. In the first chapter there is mention of a German monument made out of artillery shells, this shows a tradition of incorporating shells in the construction of monuments in Gavrelle. The battlefield debris, even though the metal originally comes from Britain and Germany, can be regarded as vernacular building material.

When a building is shelled, the first thing to go is the roof and tiles. The tiles used in the village would have been the red baked type, but it was decided to use Welsh slate for the plaques because of the durability and contrast to the red brickwork. As stated before, the badges on the RND monument on the Ancre were too small and these had to be larger, the size of the regimental badges on the CWGC headstones. The CWGC have about 1500 stencil badges which they use for this purpose, but this does not include the badges of the Naval Battalions as all six naval battalions are represented by the Divisional badge of the fouled admiralty anchor. Therefore, these had to be made the size of CWGC regimental badges placed on the new RND memorial. The six different naval badges are on the left of the doorway and a RMLI badge on the right of the doorway represents 1/RMLI and 2/RMLI who sustained so many casualties around the Windmill. On the wall facing the road to Gavrelle are the plaques of the four army service battalion badges. Inside the monument, under the anchor, symbolically holding it, is a plaque to the 14/Worcesters, the RND pioneers. With a classical monument you naturally 'stand back', but with this monument, in a unique way, you can enter inside the destroyed house. The roof is gone but, as with so many of the villages fortified in the Great War, the concrete you are standing on is not the base of the monument but simply a roof of a symbolic dugout or reinforced cellar.

The monument was financed mainly from donations from Royal Naval Associations and Royal Marine Association Branches but other organisations and individuals also contributed to the cost of the brickwork and plaques.

The building of the 1984 by-pass created a small triangular strip of land between the old road and new by-pass. This strip of redundant land was then considered as a possible site. The site is called a 'park of peace and remembrance' and it is hoped to acquire the land next to the site to convert into a turnabout car park. The land was made available because of road improvements but the site is exposed to the noisy traffic, and plans are proceeding to have a hedge between the N50 and the Memorial. Another future plan is to have the north west inside corner bricked off and a box container with door fitted to hold a visitors' book (and the cemetery register for Naval Trench Cemetery).

When the Gulf War ended in February 1991 the temporarily postponed dedication ceremony was reinstated and the memorial was dedicated on 5 May 1991. The guard of honour was provided by a contingent from the local regiment based at Arras and the ship's company of HMS Dragon (a RNR communication training shore establishment from Swansea), sadly now decommissioned.

THE MEMORIAL TO ABBE PIERRE CARPENTIER (1912-1943)

The memorial to Pierre Carpentier was erected in the communal cemetery and was dedicated on 8 May 1995, the 50th Anniversary of the ending of the war in Europe. Carpentier was a man of peace and war, and wore a military uniform as well as a cassock. He worked with the French Resistance in gathering information, and helping evaders and escapees to return back to Britain. He was betrayed in December 1942, deported to Germany and beheaded in 1943.

Pierre Carpentier was born in Libercourt (east of Lens) on 2 July 1912. He would have been just over two years old when the Germans arrived in October 1914; his younger

Sketch of sous-lieutenant Pierre Carpentier, 51st Infantry Regiment.

183

sister was born a few weeks after the invasion.

Pierre was six years old when the Great War ended and with life back to normal he concentrated on his education. He studied at Cambrai College and one of his baccalauréat subjects was German.

Since the early age of 4 or 5 Pierre took an interest in his religion, which was encouraged by l'abbé Mouchelin of Roeux. His other great love was scouting and he became a scout leader. In 1932 Pierre went to Amiens to study as a priest, was ordained on 29 June 1938 in Amiens Cathedral and was allocated to a parish in Abbeville.

Military service was compulsory in France, and Pierre was called up, offered a commission and sent to the main military college. When mobilised in 1939 he was a sous-lieutenant in the 13 Company Pioneers of the 51st Regiment. After the fall of France in June 1940 Pierre went back to his parish in Abbeville to find his church, l'église Saint-Gilles, in ruins, along with most of Abbeville, which had been in the path of the Panzer divisions when they raced to the coast, then up to Boulogne, Calais and Dunkerque.

At the fall of France, France was divided into two; the part the Germans held and Vichy France to the south. In the valuable industrial north, restriction of movement was imposed; the border of this *Zone dite Interdite* was the Somme River which ran through Abbeville. Pierre Carpentier's parish was in a very important position in the route of escapees and evaders. An evader is someone that has not yet been caught and after the fall of France there were an estimated 2000-3000 British soldiers that had not been rounded up by the Germans; most of these went back to the French families they were billeted with. Some were captured, some were sheltered by French families. (In Arleux communal cemetery, for example, there is a private of the 2/Cameronians [Scottish Rifles] who died in October 1940, buried near his comrades of the 22 May 1940. Was he taken in wounded but died months later?) Hundreds of the BEF, however, made it through the quickly organised escape route, which included Pierre Carpentier, who provided travel documents with the help of a small printing press. This priest, unfortunately, was betrayed by a British sergeant of the BEF. The story of Sergeant Harold Cole is not a pleasant one but it has to be told.

Harold Cole was born in east London in January 1906. His father, Albert Cole in the 11/West Yorks, was wounded in the Battle of the Somme, and died of wounds back in Blighty in August 1916 and is buried in Chingford Mount Cemetery, Essex. Harold Cole was only 10½ when his father died in the Great War. His mother soon married again and they moved to another part of London, and Harold soon got a reputation as a petty criminal, even while still at school. With youthful energy and some charisma he was known as 'Sonny Boy', a cheeky, cockney, confidence trickster.

When the Second World War broke out, Cole found himself in the army. He was becoming too well known in east London, and the army presented a new life and new opportunities. With his natural ability to masquerade and influence, he very soon became a sergeant and went to France with 18 Company of the Royal Engineers, and was billeted in the suburbs of Lille. Cole spent the 'Phony

War' in northern France, helping to build ferro-concrete pillboxes along the Franco-Belgian border.

This new life and different country did not change Cole's old ways, and he was soon caught stealing from the Sergeants' Mess. While in captivity awaiting trial he escaped (another one of his talents), but was later arrested in a hotel room in Lens.

The Germans invaded France on 10 May 1940. In the general retreat to Dunkerque, Cole took advantage of the chaos and once again escaped. To return to Britain was the last thing Cole wanted but surviving in a foreign country under occupation was not going to be easy. Cole's petty criminal background provided him with many talents, which he exploited. He was not the only BEF member left in France and, after the fall of France, the RAF relentlessly attacked coastal France to hamper Hitler's invasion plans, which resulted in many downed aviators. These trained aircrew were valuable to the war effort, if only they could get back to Britain.

When the escape routes were formed, Cole took this opportunity and passed himself off as a British officer in France working for MI9. He got many soldiers and airmen out of the country and operated in France with very little problem. He spoke atrocious French (with a cockney accent), but he obtained a medical certificate to say he had a speech and hearing problem. Cole was the master of the double-bluff. The Germans were looking for people who were trying to blend into the crowd, so Cole did the opposite and attracted attention to himself (and the person he was trying to smuggle out of the country), so the Germans generally paid little attention to this inarticulate attention seeker and his rather embarrassed associate.

As with all frauds, it was only a matter of time before he was found out. Resistance funds were not distributed by Cole but spent on himself. In one incident it was found that a supposed Polish fighter pilot he was trying to smuggle out was just an ordinary Polish refugee who had paid Cole a great deal of money to get him to Britain. After about a year the Germans also realised what he was doing and arrested him. Unfortunately Cole would do anything to save his own skin and started working for the Germans, and slowly betrayed his comrades, one of them being Abbé Pierre Carpentier.

Cole was in Germany when the war was coming to an end, so he made his way to the Swiss border but en route was captured by the Americans. Always trying to con his way out of trouble, he told the advancing Americans he was a British secret agent and, with the information that only an agent (or traitor) would know, he once again talked himself out of trouble, and even started working with the Americans to find Nazis who had gone underground. He had once again turned things around; now the hunted was the hunter. However, when a suspected Nazi died in interrogation (Cole was after Nazi gold not a confession), he was on the run again. Wanted by the British, French and Americans, he was caught just after the war but once again escaped from a military prison and his end finally came in January 1946 in a shoot-out with French police in his room over a cafe in Paris. He was buried in an unmarked grave just outside of Paris.

Chapter Eleven

BRIEF HISTORY OF THE ROYAL NAVAL DIVISION

This Division was a unique formation, which until September 1916 was known as the Royal Naval Division (RND). It was formed in 1914 on the outbreak of the war using surplus Naval Reservists. The concept of a naval field force was not a new one, there had been naval brigades in the Sudan Campaign of the mid 1880s and again in the Boer War. The admiralty had plans for a Royal Marine Brigade, basically as a landing force to seize ports. This force could only act as a raiding or spearhead force as the Royal Marines lacked artillery, engineering and all the logistics of an army division. On the outbreak of war, however, there were more men than boats, enough surplus reservists, predominantly stokers, to form one division of infantry. One brigade was formed of Royal Marines and the other two were Naval Reservists. Their officer corps was composed of gifted men, men who were artistic and academic mixed with genuinely skilled men looking for adventure.

Amongst these were Rupert Brooke, Arthur Asquith, Bernard Freyberg and A.P. Herbert. The other ranks consisted of RNVR men, Royal Marines and Stokers, and a large contingent of recruits who could barely fire a rifle. This Division was under Admiralty command with naval ranks, customs and uniforms, its battalions were even named after admirals. The Division was sent to Belgium in October 1914 to assist the Belgians around Antwerp but after a short while was withdrawn, losing a third of its strength interned in Holland or taken prisoner. On return to Britian, there was a scandal as to why such an ill prepared unit was sent abroad. Some sailors had one water bottle between two, school satchels were bought from suppliers in the southeast to give the men some sort of webbing, many even lacked overcoats; it was not a good beginning.

The Division was reconstituted with new recruits from all over the country, with contingents from the RNVR depots of Tyne, Clyde, Wales, London, Bristol, Mersey and Sussex. It formed its own depot at Blandford in Dorset and started training in earnest. The Division was run on the Guards system, having its own depot to supply its battalions. Once a man was allocated a battalion, he would serve with that throughout the war, which was contrary to the practice in the rest of the army. This gave the recruit a real sense of

Recruiting poster for the RND. The Benbow and Collingwood disbanded after losses at Gallipoli.

belonging to the unit. The Division took part in the Gallipoli campaign where it suffered many casualties; after its withdrawal from Gallipoli the Division was kept garrisoning the Aegean Islands whilst it's future was discussed. It was decided to disband the Division, the duration only RNVR men were to be transferred to the army or sea service, and the Marines back to sea service. At the last moment, in mid April whilst undergoing disbandment, the Royal Naval Division was reprieved, reconstituted, and ordered to France. There were to be several changes, though. The new recruits were to be supplied from the War Office, and trained in the Division's own depot. The Division itself would come under the command of the War Office, but naval ranks and conditions of service applied. Lastly only two of the brigades were to be of naval personnel with the third Brigade composed of army units; the Division would also gets its own artillery at last.

A sailor of the Collingwood Battalion. There is a monument to the Collingwood Battalion at Blandford in Dorest.

The Army resented the RND because of its unorthodox attitude and there were many attempts to break it. The first attempt came when its commanding officer, Major-General Paris of the Royal Marines Artillery, was seriously wounded in October 1916. His replacement was General Shute, who took a dislike to his new charges and doubted their ability. The RND was renumbered the 63rd (RN) Division, and its brigades numbered 188, 189 and 190, to conform with the army order of battle. The RND got a chance to prove itself at the tail end of the Somme campaign when, together with the 51st Highland Division, who also had its abilities doubted, they confounded their critics with spectacular success around Beaumont Hamel and Beaucourt, during which Bernard Freyberg of Hood Battalion, RND, gained the Victoria Cross. The RND had established a good fighting reputation but at a fearful cost. The Division was withdrawn to refit and rebuild, with the first batch of army supplied conscripts coming in.

The Division had a unique esprit de corps, and was constantly having to fight the Army as well as the Germans for its survival. The Division fought around the Ancre in February, pushing the line forward before the Germans abandoned their lines and withdrew in March. The RND was moved down to the Arras sector for the Arras offensive and ready for their date with

RND Christmas Card 1916. This cartoon shows the RND using their naval skills to survive the sea of mud of trench warfare. 'Up Anchor' is a pun on the River Ancre, where they spent Christmas that year.

A group of RMLI at Blandford Camp, late 1916.

history at Gavrelle. This guide gives an account of the Gavrelle fighting. This action was a defining moment in the Royal Naval Division as it was at Gavrelle that almost the last of the originals were killed off, those Gallipoli survivors and those who had just come back from wounds incurred at Beaucourt. Gavrelle was the deathbed of the original RND. The division was rebuilt with men who had inherited a reputation which they enhanced at Poelcappele, Welsh Ridge, the Somme in March 1918 and on the final advance to victory when it breached the Queant-Drocourt line, the Canal du Nord, and with the 57th Division, helped capture Cambrai, feats that are commonly only credited to the Canadians, alongside whom they fought. It is not fashionable to praise British formations. The Division was disbanded in early 1919, never to reform, so became a wartime only formation, but what a legacy they left us. During its short history it gained six VCs and suffered 45000 casualties.

A group of matelots and marines at their galley.

BIBLIOGRAPHY

First World War

Barnes, B.S., *This Righteous War*, Richard Netherwood Ltd, 1990

Blumberg, H.E., *Britain's Sea Soldiers*, Swiss & Co., 1925

Cave, Nigel, *Vimy Ridge: Arras*, Leo Cooper, Battleground Europe, 1996

Cohen, J., *Journey to the Trenches, Life of Isaac Rosenburg 1890-1918,* Robson Books, 1974

Edmonds, James, *Military Operations France and Belgium, 1918, Vol. II,* Imperial War Museum Books, 1937

Falls, Cyril, *Military Operations France and Belgium 1917, Vol. I,* Imperial War Museum Books, 1940

Franks, Norman, *Who Downed the Aces in WW1?* Grub Street, 1996

Franks, Bailey & Duiven, *The Jasta War Chronology,* Grub Street, 1998

Gibbons, Floyd, *The Red Knight of Germany,* Cassel, 1927

Gibson & Oldfield, *Sheffield City Battalion,* Wharncliffe Publishing, 1988

Goold Walker, G., *The Honourable Artillery Company in the Great War*, Seeley, Service & Co., 1930

Haig & Turner, (Editors), *The Long Carry: Journal of Frank Dunham,* Pergamon Press, 1970

Henshaw, Trevor, *The Sky Their Battlefield*, Grub Street, 1995

Jerrold, Douglas, *The Royal Naval Division,* Hutchinson, 1927

Kilduff, Peter, *Richthofen: Beyond the Legend of the Red Baron,* Arms and Armour, 1994

Macksey, Kenneth, *The Shadow of Vimy Ridge,* William Kimber, 1965

Middlebrook, Martin, (Editor), *The Diaries of Horace Bruckshaw RMLI,* 1979

Mitchinson, K.W., *Gentlemen and Officers,* Imperial War Museum Books, 1995

Moyer, L., *Victory Must Be Ours, Germany and the Great War,* Leo Cooper, 1995

Murray, Joseph, *Call to Arms,* William Kimber, 1980

Nicholls, Jonathan, *Cheerful Sacrifice,* Leo Cooper, 1990

Page, C., *Command in the Royal Naval Division: Biography of Brigadier General Asquith,* Spellmount, 1999

Saunders, Anthony, *Weapons of the Trench War 1914-1918*, Sutton Publishing, 1999

Sellers, Leonard, *The Hood Battalion,* Leo Cooper, 1995

Stewart & Sheen, *Tyneside Scottish,* Pen & Sword Books, 1999

Second World War

Chorley, W.R., *Bomber Command Losses,* WW2, Vol. V, 1997

Coilliot, André, *Quatre longues annéens d'occupation,* Beaurains, 1985

Cossey, Bob, *Tigers: The Story of No. 74 Squadron RAF,* 1992

Cull, Lander & Weiss, *Twelve Days in May, (10-21 May 1940),* Grub Street, 1995

Ellis, L.F., *Welsh Guards at War*, Gale & Polden Ltd, 1946

Foot & Langley, MI9, *Escape and Evasion 1939-1945,* 1979

Horne, Alistair, *To Lose a Battle: May 1940,* Macmillan, 1969

Leclerc, T., *Pierre Carpentier, vicaire,* Abbeville, 1993

Murphy, B.M., *Turncoat: The Strange Case of British Traitor Sergeant Harold Cole,* Harcourt Brace Jovanovich Publishers, 1987

CWGC Cemeteries and Memorials

Longworth, Philip, *The Unending Vigil,* Secker & Warburg, 1967

Ward & Gibson, *Courage Remembered*, HMSO, 1989

For those interested in the Royal Naval Division, there is a quarterly journal called "RND" dedicated to in-depth study of this unique Division. Further details can be obtained from the editor: Leonard Sellers, 17a Bellhouse Road, Eastwood, Leigh-on-Sea, Essex, SS9 5NL.

INDEX

190